Kali Theatre and Pentabus Theatre

THE HUSBANDS

By **Sharmila Chauhan**

First public performance
12 February 2013, Plymouth Theatre Royal The Drum

'Up to 50 million girls are thought to be 'missing' over the past century due to female infanticide and foeticide' UN Population Fund

The Husbands originally began as a short story called *Frangipani Hill* that I wrote some years ago as a response to the growing problems in India arising out of female feticide (aborting females fetuses) and female infanticide (killing girl babies).

The census statistics (2011) show that in some parts of India for every 1000 boys born there are only 300 girls, and things are getting worse. Not surprisingly, the United Nations calls India one of the most dangerous places on earth for a girl.

Polyandry (where a woman has more than one husband) is an ancient practice noted as far back as the Mahabarat. It is still practised today in certain areas, where there are not enough women for men to marry, but unlike in the past, these women are subjugated and treated as servants.

In striking contrast, India has a history of matriarchal societies and Devi (Goddess worship) where Shakti (feminine energy) is believed to be a foundation of life. I found this paradox fascinating. I felt that maybe there was a disconnect between these two things; what would happen if instead of subjugating women, a new system was established that returned to ancient practices of matriarchy? Could reversing the roles make a difference? And so the premise of Shaktipur was born.

During my research I was amazed to find that communities such as the Nair women of Kerala had a centuries old system of matriarchy that also practised polyandry (in some parts). These systems are now extinct but suggest that there is within India a possibility to do things differently

These findings, that India has in itself a rich history that could be the seed to grow something different, was really inspiring. The roles of women, not just in India, are complex: often a blend of many conflicting demands and choices and this is really what Aya faces. I hope that the play says something truthful about the roles of women everywhere.

The relationships between Aya and her husbands are real – they are not abstract ideas – and I really wanted this to come through. These are personal journeys that we all struggle with. So while set in India, the themes of love, power and female sexuality also make *The Husbands* an allegory for society in the West.

Sharmila Chauhan

Kali Theatre and Pentabus Theatre

The Husbands

by Sharmila Chauhan

Aya	**Syreeta Kumar**
Sem	**Rhik Samadder**
Omar	**Mark Theodore**
Jerome	**Phillip Edgerley**

Director	**Janet Steel**
Creative Advisor	**Elizabeth Freestone**
Design	**Jean Chan**
Lighting	**Prema Mehta**
Music	**Arun Ghosh**
Movement	**Shobna Gulati**
Production Manager	**Luke Child**
Company Stage Manager	**Sarah Julie Pujol**
Technical Stage Manager	**Sam Eccles**

COMPANY BIOGRAPHIES

Sharmila Chauhan *Writer*
Theatre found Sharmila when she was pregnant. The birth of her son coincided with selection for the Royal Court's writing programme. Her play *Born Again/Purnajanam* was performed in January 2012 at Southwark Playhouse as part of *Tagore's Women* (Directed by Janet Steel of Kali). *When Spring Comes*, an exploration of the Asian Ugandan exodus, was performed in autumn 2012 (Dir: Domonic Hingorani) in conjunction with Tamasha and South Asian Lit Fest. Sharmila was twice nominated for the Asian New Writer award and her short stories have been published in print and online. She is also working on a novel. Trained as a pharmacist, with a PhD in Clinical Pharmacology, Sharmila gave up academia to follow the writer's life. Fascinated by the quiet meaning of people's lives, her work is often a transgressive meditation on love, sex and exploration of the diaspora. She lives in London with her husband, son and cat Tashi. www.sharmilathewriter.com @sci_literati

Janet Steel *Director*
Artistic Director of Kali since 2003. After many years as an actress, Janet's directing career began in 1988 at Loose Change Theatre with her first full-length piece, *White Biting Dog*. Directing: *Behzti* (The Rep), *April in Paris, Bretevski Street, A Hard Rain, Top Girls* (Northampton Royal), *Millennium Mysteries, Big School* (Belgrade Coventry); *Antigone, The Mother, Orpheus Descending, An Ideal Husband, Romeo & Juliet, The Knockey, Serious Money* (Rose Bruford). For Kali: Over 35 readings of new work and productions of *Calcutta Kosher (2004 & 2012), Chaos, Paper Thin, Deadeye, Zameen, Another Paradise, Behna, Ghandi & Coconuts, Purnjanam/Born Again, Mustafa* and *My Daughter's Trial*.

Elizabeth Freestone *Creative Advisor*
Trained at Rose Bruford College and RNT Studio. For Pentabus: *Blue Sky, Stand Up Diggers All, This Same England, The Hay Play*. Other directing includes: *The Rape of Lucrece, Here Lies Mary Spindler, The Tragedy of Thomas Hobbes, The Comedy of Errors* (RSC); *Endless Light* (Kali/Southwark Playhouse); *The Duchess of Malfi, Dr Faustus, The School for Scandal, Volpone* (Greenwich Theatre); *Romeo and Juliet* (Shakespeare's Globe); *Top Girls, Three Sisters, Night Must Fall* (RWCMD); *Skellig, Rocket Fuel, No Place Like Home* (OnO Theatre); *The Travels of the Three English Brothers* (British Museum); *A Gloriously Mucky Business* (LAMDA/Lyric Hammersmith); *The Water Harvest* (Theatre503). Associate Director on *The Caucasian Chalk Circle* (RNT) and a Staff Director at the National, the Royal Court, Hampstead Theatre and Soho Theatre.

Phillip Edgerley *Jerome*

Phillip Edgerley is an actor who has worked in all areas of the industry including work with the National Theatre, Dreamthinkspeak and the BBC. Most recently he has been working with the renowned visual artist Alexandre Singh on his play, *The Humans* which premiered in Rotterdam and New York and is due for further international performances in 2014. In 2009 he joined The RSC's Long Ensemble Company performing eight plays over two and a half years in London, Stratford and New York. Currently, he is a guest director at the London Academy of Music and Dramatic Art and Shakespeare's Globe.

Rhik Samadder *Sem*

Rhik Samadder trained at Drama Centre London. Since graduating his theatre credits include title roles in *The Indian Boy* (RSC) and *Romeo and Juliet* (Salisbury Playhouse). Other theatre includes *King Saturn* (Soho Theatre), *Fewer Emergencies* (Oxford Playhouse), *No Smoke* (Arcola Theatre) and *Ealing Common* (Theatre503). Film Credits include: *Chemical Wedding* (Warner Bros) and *Arrivals* (Wilf Varvill). TV credits include: *Strikeback* (HBO) and *Doctors* (BBC). Corporate work includes work for NHS, SANE and idents for Channel 4. Rhik is also a regular freelance journalist for the *Guardian*.
Twitter @whatsamadder

Syreeta Kumar *Aya*

Trained at the Bristol Old Vic Theatre School and has worked extensively in theatre and television. Theatre credits include Olivia in *Twelfth Night* (Filter Theatre Company), *Midnight's Children, Hamlet, Much Ado About Nothing, Camino Real* (Royal Shakespeare Company), *Haroun* and *The Sea Of Stories* (National Theatre), has also worked with London Bubble, Tara Arts, Talawa, Theatre Royal Stratford East and Leicester Haymarket. Television credits include *Silk, Torchwood, The Shadow Line, Hustle, Doctors, Eastenders* and most recently *Coronation Street*. She lives in Brighton with her two daughters, cat, dog, and ONE husband.

Mark Theodore *Omar*

Trained: Poor School. Theatre includes: *Julius Caesar* (RSC), *The Prince of Homburg* (Donmar Warehouse), *Three Sisters* (Lyric Hammersmith), *Twelfth Night* (York Theatre Royal), *Treasure Island* (West End), *Days of Significance, Macbeth, God in Ruins, Pericles, The Winter's Tale, Days of Significance* (RSC), *Festen* (National Tour), *93.2 fm* (Royal Court), *A Raisin in the Sun* (Young Vic), *Animal Farm* (Northern Stage), *Dirty Butterfly, Wrong Place* (Soho Theatre), *Measure for Measure* (NT). TV includes: *Obsession: Dark Desires* (October Films), *The Dumping Ground* (BBC), *Friday Night Dinner* (Big Talk Productions), *Julius Caesar* (Illuminations Television). Film includes: *Ali G in da House*.

Jean Chan *Set and Costume Designer*
Graduated from Royal Welsh College of Music and Drama. Trainee
Designer for the RSC. Won the 2009 Linbury Prize for Stage Design. A
runner up in the Arts Foundation Awards 2013. Design credits include:
BFG (Dundee Rep); *Tonypandemonium* (National Theatre Wales), *Hope
Light and Nowhere* (Edinburgh Fringe), *The Hairy Ape, The Irish Giant,
The Seagull* (Southwark Playhouse); *The Suit* (Young Vic); *Hamlet YPS*
(RSC); *The Garbage King* (Unicorn Theatre). *1984, Alice By Heart* (Lyric
Hammersmith); *Mayfair* (Pentabus/Latitude Festival); *I Have a Dream*
(Polka); *When The Waters Came* (Theatre Centre); *Why the Lion Danced*
(Yellow Earth Theatre); *The Birthday of the Infanta* (Trestle Theatre); *The
Roman Bath* (Arcola Theatre); Associate Design credits include: *Lionboy*
(Complicite), *Five Guys Named Moe* (Edinburgh & Theatre Royal Stratford
East); *Monsters* (Arcola /Strawberry Vale Productions). www.jeanchan.co.uk

Arun Ghosh *Sound*
Arun Ghosh is a British Asian clarinettist, composer, Musical Director and
music educator. He has composed music for over forty theatre, dance
and radio productions, and has released three critically acclaimed albums;
Northern Namaste (2008), *Primal Odyssey* (2011) and *A South Asian Suite*
(2013) on Camoci Records. Other significant works include his re-score
of feature length animation *The Adventures of Prince Achmed*, and
contemporary dance piece, *A Handful of Dust*. Arun is an Associate Artist
of The Albany, Deptford and of Spitalfields Music 2014, and was Artist in
Residence for the Alchemy Festival 2011 at the Southbank.

Prema Mehta *Lighting Designer*
Prema Mehta works as a Lighting Designer for drama and dance
productions. For Kali: *Speed* and *Twelve* (Tristan Bates Theatre), *Shared
Memories* and *Calcutta Kosher* (Arcola). Other theatre includes: *The Great
Extension* (Theatre Royal Stratford East), *Snow Queen* (Derby Theatre) and
The Electric Hills (Liverpool Everyman). Designs for dance include *Jugni*
(UK tour), *Maaya* (Westminster Hall), *Bells* (Mayor of London's Showtime)
and *Sufi Zen* (Royal Festival Hall). Forthcoming designs include *OK Tata
Tata* and *The Periera's Bakery at 76 Chapel Road* (Leicester Curve) and
Fourteen (Watford Palace). Further details at www.premamehta.com

Sarah Julie Pujol *Company Stage Manager*
Sarah is a freelance Stage Manager based in London. Recent credits
include: Company Stage Manager for *Talkback* (Kali at Tristan Bates);
Stage Manager for *Children of Fate* by Inside Intelligence (CLF Theatre);
Assistant Stage Manager for *The Old Woman* directed by Robert Wilson
(UK, Italy, Greece); Company Stage Manager for *XY* by Papercut Theatre
(Pleasance Courtyard, Edinburgh); Stage Manager for *PEEP* by Natural
Shocks (Assembly Gardens, Edinburgh); Stage Manager for *Equal Writes*
(Tristan Bates Theatre, London) and Stage Manager for *XY* by Papercut
Theatre (Theatre503, London).

Sam Eccles *Technical Stage Manager*
Graduated with BA from University of Wales Trinity St David in Theatre Design and Production. At UoW: *Fahrenheit 451, Oh What a Lovely War, Holey Matrimony*. Sam has spent six years in theatre and events as a freelance Technical Stage Manager and Lighting Designer. For Pentabus: *Milked, In This Place, For Once, Blue Sky, Underland, White Open Spaces. Tea Time* (Oxford Play House); *Venezia the Show* (Teatro San Gallo); *Dismorphia* (Sean Tuan John); Peter Pan (New Vic Theatre): *Event Lighting Design: Sheep Music Festival, Hard Rock Café Venice, OysterBand, Flight the Bear*.

Luke Child *Production Manager*
Luke has toured both in the UK and internationally with some of the most commercially successful productions including *The Lion King, The King and I, The Rocky Horror Show* and *Matthew Bourne's Dorian Gray*. One of his proudest achievements was to open a major new theatre in Dublin, where he spent two years dedicated to the venue's success. Luke is delighted to have the opportunity to work with Kali and Pentabus on *The Husbands*.

Shobna Gulati *Movement*
Theatre includes: *Dinnerladies* (Comedy Theatre tour); *Body Gossip* (Edinburgh Fringe); *Girls Night* (National tour); *The Vagina Monologues* (Mark Goucher); *Pretend You Have Big Buildings, Parminder Café Vesuvio* (Royal Exchange); *Dancing Within Walls, Crazy Lady* (Drill Hall/Contact Theatre); *Romeo and Juliet* (Leicester Haymarket); *A Midsummer Night's Dream* (Tara Arts/National tour); *How High is Up?* (West Yorkshire Playhouse); *Moti Roti Puttli Chunni* (Stratford East); *The Mahabharata* (Year of Opera); *The Sacred Thread* (Royal Festival Hall). TV includes: Sunita in *Coronation Street*, Anita in *Dinnerladies, The Circle* (Channel 4), *Eastenders*. Panellist on *Call My Bluff, Have I Got News For You, Loose Women*. Film includes BAFTA winning *Shadowscan*. Also extensive work across the UK as a choreographer and dancer. She has an honorary doctorate from The University of Huddersfield.

kalí

Intrepid plays by fearless women

Kali Theatre has been presenting ground-breaking new theatre writing by women with a South Asian background for over twenty years. They seek out and nurture strong individual writers who challenge our perceptions through original and thought-provoking drama, and actively encourage their writers to reinvent and reshape the theatrical agenda.

Their work presents the distinct perspective and experience of South Asian women, engaging people from all backgrounds in work that reflects and comments on our lives today. They have won rave reviews, sold-out shows and inspired audiences all over the UK with work that challenges our perceptions through original and surprising theatre.

"The most enjoyably inventive piece
of theatre I've seen this year"
The Guardian on *Behna*

Join our mailing list **www.kalitheatre.co.uk**
Email us **info@kalitheatre.co.uk**
Like us **www.facebook.com/KalitheatreUK**
Tweet us **@kalitheatreUK**

For Kali Theatre

Artistic Director	**Janet Steel**
General Manager	**Christopher Corner**
Admin and Marketing	**Binita Walia**
Press Representation	**Yasmeen Khan**

Board: **Shelley King (Chair), Amy Beeson, Elizabeth Cuffy, Penny Gold, Alison McFadden, Anouk Mishti, Rozet Shah, Shiroma Silva, Jocelyn Watson, Elizabeth Youard**

Charity no: 1071733

Supported using public funding by
ARTS COUNCIL ENGLAND

Purnjanam 2012

Mustafa 2012

Sock 'em With Honey 2002

Chaos 2005

Ghandhi and Coconuts 2010

Calcutta Kosher 2012

Zameen 2008

Photos: Robert Workman, Robert Day

PENTABUS THEATRE

Pentabus is a contemporary theatre company, touring new plays about the rural world.

We produce plays that dig deep into the psyche of the English countryside. Shows are playful, political and compassionate, offering rural audiences theatre made especially for, and that speaks directly to, them. We then take these plays on the road, telling stories that are born locally, but resonate nationally.

In challenging times for the rural world, Pentabus brings front-line reports from forgotten communities, telling stories that matter for and about the contemporary countryside.

Pentabus turns 40 in 2014. The company was founded in 1974 and originally toured to five counties in the Midlands, hence PENT (five) and BUS (touring). Today we tour new plays all over the country. Recent productions include *Milked* by Simon Longman, about rural unemployment and a cow called Sandy, *In This Place* by Lydia Adetunji and Frances Brett, about women working in the countryside, *For Once* by Tim Price about teenagers and market towns, *Stand Up Diggers All* by Phil Porter exploring the links between the Occupy movement and land reclamation; and *Blue Sky* by Clare Bayley, about isolated rural airports.

Our productions turn up at festivals, in fields, in village halls and in theatres, reaching our audience wherever they may be. In fact, our mission can be summed up as: we tell the most exciting stories in the most surprising ways.

This Theatre has the support of the Channel 4 Playwright's scheme sponsored by Channel 4 Television.

Pentabus Theatre, Bromfield, Ludlow, Shropshire, SY8 2JU
www.pentabus.co.uk

Follow us on Twitter @pentabustheatre
Find us on Facebook - Pentabus Theatre

Pentabus is a registered charity, number 287909.

We rely on the generosity of our donors, small and large, to help us to continue to deliver more arts projects in new ways. You can read more and donate online at www.justgiving.org.uk/pentabustheatre

For Pentabus

Artistic Director	Elizabeth Freestone
Managing Director	Rachael Griffin
Administrator	Sarah Hughes
Bookkeeper	Lynda Lynne
Technical Manager	Sam Eccles
Channel 4 Playwright	Simon Longman

Board of Directors

Kate Organ (Chair), Joseph Alford, Richard Burbidge, Ed Collier, Sean Holmes, Diane Lenan, Karen McLellan, Jamie Perry, Elanor Thompson, Lyndsey Turner, Mary Wells and Alison Vermee

Supported using public funding by
ARTS COUNCIL ENGLAND
LOTTERY FUNDED

Actress Dominique Bull as Ana from *Blue Sky* by Clare Bayley
photo credit Robert Workman (photo entitled ana with torch)

Actors Adam Redmore and Oliver Mott as Paul and Snowy from *Milked* by Simon Longman
photo credit Robert Stanton

Audience Member experiencing *In This Place* by Lydia Adetunji and Frances Brett
photo credit Florence Fox

21 Dean Street,
London W1D 3NE
Admin 020 7287 5060
Box Office 020 7478 0100
www.sohotheatre.com

London's most vibrant venue for new theatre, comedy and cabaret.

Soho Theatre is a major creator of new theatre, comedy and cabaret. Across our three different spaces we curate the finest live performance we can discover, develop and nurture. Soho Theatre works with theatre makers and companies in a variety of ways, from full producing of new plays, to co-producing new work, working with associate artists and presenting the best new emerging theatre companies that we can find. We have numerous writers and theatre makers on attachment and under commission, six young writers and comedy groups and we read and see hundreds of shows a year – all in an effort to bring our audience work that amazes, moves and inspires. We attract over 170,000 audience members a year.

'Soho Theatre was buzzing, and there were queues all over the building as audiences waited to go into one or other of the venue's spaces. [The audience] is so young, exuberant and clearly anticipating a good time.' *Guardian*

We produced, co-produced or staged over forty new plays in the last twelve months.

Our social enterprise business model means that we maximise value from Arts Council and philanthropic funding; we actually contribute more to government in tax and NI than we receive in public funding.

Soho Theatre relies upon the generosity of its audience, Soho Theatre Friends, and donations from a whole range of people and organisations to support its artistic programme and charitable activities. To find out more about how you can help please visit our website. You can see a list of our current supporters in the box office lobby and also on our website. We also wish to thank those supporters who wish to stay anonymous, as well as all of our Soho Theatre Friends.

sohotheatre.com

Keep up to date
sohotheatre.com/mailing-list
facebook.com/sohotheatre
twitter.com/sohotheatre

SOHO STAFF

THE HUSBANDS

Sharmila Chauhan

THE HUSBANDS

OBERON BOOKS
LONDON

WWW.OBERONBOOKS.COM

First published in 2014 by Oberon Books Ltd

521 Caledonian Road, London N7 9RH

Tel: +44 (0) 20 7607 3637 / Fax: +44 (0) 20 7607 3629

e-mail: info@oberonbooks.com

www.oberonbooks.com

PB ISBN: 978-1-78319-113-0

E ISBN: 978-1-78319-612-8

Cover design by Luke Wakeman

Printed, bound and converted
by CPI Group (UK) Ltd, Croydon, CR0 4YY.

Visit www.oberonbooks.com to read more about all our books and to buy them. You will also find features, author interviews and news of any author events, and you can sign up for e-newsletters so that you're always first to hear about our new releases.

Acknowledgements

Greatest thanks to the Higher Spirits for guidance.

For Courttia for your unwavering love, support and inspiration. Thanks for being the light on stormy days. My parents – Tara and Arvind for your kindness and love always: and of course unlimited babysitting. Sunil for being a listening ear and fellow writer in the family. Senen – you have already taught me the hardest and best lessons in life.

Janet and Elizabeth – without you none of this would be possible. Thank you for believing in me and my writing. Anjum who saw the potential and helped me with those first drafts. Anita, you were there from the beginning; thank you. Ramona whose look of gratitude after seeing the first reading kept me writing in the hard times. Anthony – for walking the path with me. Tian for listening to my rants and laments patiently. Olu and Mik: we are the Critical Mass! Fleur – your hugs! Goldy for your generosity of spirit and belief. Anjuli – for love and support – even from afar.

Thanks Rhik, Mark, Syreeta and Philip – you guys are inspiring. The production team and everyone at Kali and Pentabus and especially Binita, Chris and Sarah.

This play is dedicated to girls whose lives have been lost or never lived. Inside the problem, lies the seed of the solution.

"She took men to the well and brought them back thirsty."

Mohammad Rasoulof
The White Meadows (2012)

Aya leads a matriarchal community in Kerala, South India called Shaktipur. This rural community was set up about fifty years ago, as a response to diminishing number of girls in India as a consequence of increasing levels of female feticide and infantacide. Here women practice polyandry, marrying several times – enabling most men to have a partner if they wish and also help to readdress the number of girls.

Aya is happily married with two husbands Sem and Omar. A young leader of the community she has plans to expand Shaktipur and take it to the city of Mumbai. Radical and decisive, she wants to take the principles of the society beyond its current reach and help women throughout India. Her new marriage to a man from resident Mumbai is her first step in this direction. She is full of hope and desire to spread her word.

But all is not well, Sem and Omar, are unsettled; concerned what this man will do to their relationship with Aya. Each loves her with his own intensity. Then as the wedding draws closer, Aya makes the discovery that may throw everything she has built up in jeopardy.

Characters

AYA

Wife and householder. Aya is an Indian woman in her mid-thirties. Enigmatic, intelligent and sensual: Aya is eternally graceful and in command.

SEM

Sweet looking, sensitive Indian man in his late twenties. He has a boyish manner. Sem is a traditional thinker and believer of the community. He is the brother of Aya's first husband Shai who passed away about seven years ago. Sem wants Aya to have a baby, but also continue the work of Shaktipur and expand it. He believes in all the principles of the community and was born into it.

OMAR

Handsome male in his mid-late 30s. Omar was born by the coast, outside Shaktipur and when he married, he brought his mother with him. Sensual and strong willed, he has an easy, self-assured manner, although is quick tempered. Omar was not born into the community, but he does his best to obey the customs since his own sister had been killed when he was a boy. Omar's father has remained at the coast, and so he often returns there. He wants Aya to have a baby and settle down and stop working so much.

JEROME

Older, 50-something European (probably English but could be French) man. Attractive and charming, he is an academic whose research takes him to India. He is a mentor and friend to Aya. Occasionally they sleep together. Since he divorced from his wife a year ago, his feelings for Aya have magnified. He has come to the village to 'save' Aya from this latest marriage and secretly wants her to give the life up and come away with him.

LANGUAGE

The language of the play is lyrical at times and the speech has a rhythm. Where characters talk over one another it is denoted by a /

LOCATION

A large two storey Keralan house. It has a veranda and rooftop terrace. There is a central courtyard where the frangipani tree resides. Behind the house are a series of outhouses and to the east the barns where the animals are kept.

Set in India there should be a feeling of intense light and heat overall.

There is also the shadow of a frangipani (champa) tree that often falls into both rooms. There should be the smell of frangipani at different times of the day set off by incense sticks.

The World of Shaktipur

Set in Southern India, most likely Kerala about fifty years from now.

Shaktipur is large community of about 5,000 people. It has been set up by wealthy north Indian women who felt a need to return to traditional values of matriarchy once prevalent in the South of India. The community is gated and protected by guards to prevent the girls being kidnapped. It is completely self sufficient – although does trade with the 'outside' and people are free to come and go as they please. The community is prosperous and harvests are bountiful. Both men and women are educated. Aya has recently (about six months ago) become the leader of Shaktipur.

Villagers each have their own land where they build their homes and grow vegetables and keep animals. Most of the land is owned by women and passed through a matrilineal line. Sons /husbands are given a share in order that they can be independent if need be. Women live with their mothers until they set up house with their husbands.

The key philosophies of the community are the worship of the Hindu Goddesses (in particular Kali) and increasing the number of girls born in order to create a community with a healthy balance of boys and girls.

The villagers are very religious – women and Goddesses are highly regarded in society. Daily running and decisions about the village are determined by the Council (all women) but the Leader is the centerpiece of village life and is looked upon to the lead the way by example.

The community has been successful economically (through trading of rice and other vegetables and spices) and in terms of progeny. There has been a small increase in the number of women to men, but polyandry is still the norm. Women are urged to take more than one husband where possible and have as many children as possible. In order to prevent abuse, it is standard practice that a woman can only take another husband if she is not, at the time of the wedding, pregnant.

The aim of Shaktipur is to grow. Aya's main fear is that if she does not engage the urban community, the ideas will be lost and never gain international support. She wants to 'pollinate' the rest of India with its ideals by creating satellite projects. Aya's fiancé has promised Aya land in Mumbai so she can carry on her work.

ACT ONE

SCENE 1: THE DAWN BREAKS

Opening festival night. Loud music, laughter. Dancing.

Fade: darkness. Sound of AYA walking (she is wearing ankle bells). Sound of tap running, then turned off. Ankle bells slowly fading into silence

Lights up: Kitchen. Just before dawn. SEM and OMAR sit on the floor. OMAR is washing lentils in a large wooden bowl. SEM is sorting through them on a large circular basket. Religious music plays faintly in the distance. The men bob their heads to it. The air is tired but festive. The music stops and there is a sound of a prayer bell ringing. Throughout this scene the men sort through (clean) and wash the lentil to a rhythm.

A statue of a pregnant Goddess forms a shrine, next to an old fashioned scale that is laden with gold coins on one side and silver on the other. The silver side is heaviest.

SEM: Listen….

> *OMAR looks up.*

They've begun…

> *SEM stands by the window looking out. The music heightens then fades.*

The Priestess is on her way to the temple.

> *SEM bows his head briefly into a Namaste.*

OMAR: Oh Kali-ma bring the night as fast as you can!

SEM: *(Teasing.)* We've just begun the fast and already you think of eating!

OMAR: Water is not enough to keep a man going…

> *SEM returns to the cleaning.*

SEM: Perhaps not, but that is the point
We sacrifice to ask for the Goddess for a blessing…
For something special

OMAR: Is there something you will be fasting for?

SEM: My reasons are the same as everyone else's:

The health of my wife, the abundance of harvest.

OMAR: And for yourself?

SEM: This is not the time for that.

OMAR shakes his head smiling.

OMAR: What a life?

Last night we ate and drunk to our fill,

Now we fast and make pious.

Tonight when the sun is gone

We throw away our restraint and eat like pigs again…

SEM: It is a time for thanks and celebration is it not brother?

OMAR: Yes it is.

But the extremes, the pretense of purity…

SEM: You think too much!

SEM grins and slowly empties his bowl of lentils into a bigger pot on the stove.

OMAR: And you, what do you believe?

SEM: Tonight we will feast and forget our worries.

People will dance and sing.

Celebrate new marriages…

Be content with our own

OMAR: Content?

OMAR stretches out onto the floor, vaguely annoyed but fighting to conceal it.

SEM: Hey brother!

He slaps him affectionately on the back

Come on, there's work to do!

OMAR: How can you work with such little sleep?

SEM: It's better to keep the mind busy so the stomach stays quiet…

OMAR: Ha!

You may be working but you are as slow as an old man!

SEM: That wine was very sweet

OMAR: Too sweet!

OMAR begins to sing something, making fun of SEM being drunk the night before. SEM ignores him, but smiles a little. He sits back down and they continue working. OMAR hums, and returns to his chores.

SEM: I wasn't drunk!

You were the one with liquor pumping through his veins!

And who was that you were dancing with last night?

OMAR: *(Off hand.)* Acquaintance

SEM tuts.

OMAR: Dancing is what the festival is all about

The women flirting with boys

Courting the men

SEM: *(Raising his eyebrows.)* And the dancing with desire?

You know the lawyer's daughter is no acquaintance.

Perhaps you were discussing council politics?

OMAR: Ah yes, the swelling of numbers,

but still the lack of girls and the need for more space…

(Laughing.)

But a festival is no time for such serious issues

SEM: Be careful brother…

OMAR: You worry too much.

A little dancing

Some talking…

The pleasure of flirtation is like those first few raindrops that catch you before you reach home

SEM: Sometimes you may not realise how wet you have become…

OMAR: The shelter of home is more comforting after becoming a little damp

SEM: Brother, you know how people talk…

OMAR: There is no one to talk *here*

Is there brother?

SEM: Someone will tell Aya

She will be angry

OMAR: Then she should have come!

SEM: She wasn't well

OMAR: Aya is never too sick for dancing…

SEM stands up and gets some more lentils. Contemplative they work in a synchronized manner throughout this conversation, forming a rhythm as they clean the lentils on large baskets.

OMAR: Tell me what did Mother say?

SEM: When?

OMAR: When she danced with you?

SEM: For the few moments before she got tired and needed to sit down?

OMAR: But tell me, what did she say?

You talked long into the night

SEM: What does a mother-in-law say?

She asked after Aya

Why she didn't attend her first festival as Leader

OMAR: Mother knows Aya does not care for traditions

SEM: Aya cares about the *right traditions*

Marriage and the works of motherhood/

OMAR: So business as usual?

SEM: Mother is not afraid of talking business during the festival

OMAR laughs.

OMAR: So she didn't proposition you?

SEM: Brother!

OMAR: *(Laughing.)* What? It wouldn't be the first time…

SEM: *(Blushing.)* Don't speak of Mother like that

OMAR: The beautiful mother of Aya – why shouldn't she desire you?

SEM: Mother was asking what we would cook

OMAR: *(Groaning, clasping stomach.)* Ah stop!

Even talking of food makes my stomach's whispers turn into shouts!

Are you so deaf you can not hear yours?

SEM: *(Presses his hand on his belly.)* Of course I hear mine

But my body is a horse

And my mind the carriage

I do not let them run away from me

OMAR: *(Looking weak.)* Perhaps mine are weak and poorly bridled

SEM: You simply need to shout a little harder

If need be, use your whip

OMAR: You tell me that tomorrow morning, when you have a sore head and an empty pocket

SEM: My horses are only bridled until sundown. Even then they are still loyal

OMAR: Not loyal enough

(Beat.)

You are the least cautious after your first sip of wine

SEM: *(Knowing this is true.)* There are times when even the horse must rein free a little

OMAR: *(Laughing.)* Indeed!

Like a child who

Is kept too close to her mother

SEM: Children always have their fathers

OMAR: Indeed. But I will watch your horses tonight

The music has stopped and the sound of birds chirping increases. Dawn is coming.

The lentils are ready. OMAR lounges back as if to sleep again. SEM pours them a glass of water each.

SEM: Brother, you can not complain of tiredness

You went to Aya's bed

OMAR: She asked me!

SEM: She always asks you!

(Beat.)

Brother, help me prepare the spices for the lamb…

OMAR relents. They measure out spices.

OMAR: I have asked Aya if I can do the sacrifice

SEM: I would do it if she asked me

OMAR: Are you so intent on punishing yourself?

SEM: I can manage…

OMAR: You nursed the lamb, fed her…

No brother, you can not kill her

SEM: *(Quickly.)* Aya will decide of course

SEM returns to work.

OMAR: So what did you tell her?

SEM: About?

OMAR: What you will cook brother…?

SEM: Translucent golden onions

Tender, seasoned, flesh

Notes of chilli, ginger

A harmony that will be our song!

OMAR smiles broadly and SEM slowly returns his grin. SEM looks out the frangipani tree in the courtyard.

SEM: And tonight the flowers will blossom, filling the air with their heady scent.

And we will celebrate, give thanks for our wife and ask for strength for the changes ahead…

Lights up as the dawn breaks.

SEM: Brother, come and look

The flowers catch the light and seem to glow

OMAR: What's that flash of green around the horizon?

AYA enters; enigmatic, graceful and beautiful. A confident smile on her face.

AYA: It comes at this time of year

The green before the day

SEM: The sky becomes the earth for a brief moment

Loving is becoming

AYA smiles at OMAR and reaches out her hand.

AYA: Some say that if the sky forgets to do this

The earth will reject the dawn

And it will be night forever more

SEM: *(Melancholic.)* But how could the sky ever forget?

AYA looks at both of them, gently smiling.

AYA: *(To OMAR.)* But you my love, are mostly sleeping when this happens, so you always miss it

OMAR: Because I am mostly tired my love.

Exhausted

OMAR walks towards her and grasps her around the waist, pulling her close. He kisses her tenderly on the lips.

SEM: Tea Aya?

AYA nods, breaking away from OMAR who watches her as she walks around the kitchen inspecting pots and pans. She stops and then gives SEM her full attention.

AYA: And you my darling, I hope you have slept and not worked all night?

SEM clears the table. OMAR places some food on it for AYA's breakfast and then sits down, pouring two glasses of water.

SEM: I slept Aya. I slept well.

AYA: Good…

And your clothes for today?

Did the tailor alter them for you?

SEM: He did.

But it's not for me to/

AYA: *(Smiling, teasing.)* Outshine the bride?

SEM looks downcast for a moment.

AYA: The two most handsome husbands in the village

How proud I am to have you both

With this, both men prostrate themselves. AYA tries to stop them and lifts them up to embrace her.

AYA: A custom, but we don't *have to* follow it in this house.

SEM: But we must Aya.

Today we must follow everything

AYA: No.

Not every rule,

Or every-'*thing*' should be followed.

She strokes both of their heads and smiles. Then spots a box of sweets (meetay) by the scales.

AYA: What is this?

SEM: The Banker has had a daughter

AYA: When?

SEM: The Husbands came early to announce it

OMAR: All *four* of them?

SEM: *(Smiling.)* They had a girl.

OMAR: So are they all taking credit?

SEM: Brother, leave them to their petty squabbles.

What does it matter whose child it is?

SEM puts the box of sweets by the shrine and gives thanks to the Goddess statue. OMAR follows suit.

AYA: A child born on this Festival day will be most blessed

AYA sits down in front of the scales and takes out a bag of coins – she takes a piece of gold from the bag and hands it to SEM.

AYA: Take it to the house Sem

Give them my congratulations

SEM: Now we have seventy girls under five

AYA places a gold coin onto the scales.

AYA: It is an achievement

(Beat.)

But not enough

SEM: But it is a start is it not?

AYA: *(Uneasy. Changing the subject.)*

Yes, of course

Let us discuss the duties for the day

Is everything in order?

SEM: Of course Aya.

AYA: Sem will the masala be ready by lunchtime?

SEM: Before the sacrifice… Of course Aya

AYA: Omar you have brought in the vegetables?

OMAR: The crops for this year's festival are good.

AYA: *(Teasing.)* It's because you haven't been at the coast so much

OMAR: My father says his fishing has suffered because I didn't come…

But I told him…/

AYA: /This is your home now.

Where you and your mother live.

He must understand this by now?

The man lives miles away and then complains when your mother takes another husband!

What does he expect?!

(Beat.)

Have you asked him to come tonight?

OMAR nods.

AYA: Good. He has a good face

Earnest, loyal

I like to see him

…

But, it is not for your father you go

You miss the sea…

Perhaps your/

Freedom?

SEM: This is a freedom in its own way

OMAR: The water… Not the life.

AYA: Still, the harvest looks all the better for your attention.

As do I my love.

SEM: With the lamb, it will be a true feast tonight.

AYA: We will need to pick flowers for the garlands.

Then others for the petals on the path and for the ceremonies.

OMAR: In the morning they will be a sludge of brown and white.

Pounded by the feet of many lost dancing until dawn…

Last harvest we danced for two days remember Aya?

AYA: *(Uncomfortable.)* I am not so young anymore…

(Beat.)

I am sure there are many others who will want to dance with you tonight

OMAR: *(Hurt.)* If my feet are found by another

It is only because yours walked away…

AYA sighs. She looks through the letters again.

AYA: Have those boys been stealing from the mango trees again?

OMAR: They're only boys, having fun

AYA: That's what they say 'outside'.

In the 'world'

Outside, Mumbai, Delhi, Chennai

Just boys *having fun*, and see what happened.

OMAR: This is not the same thing

AYA: How am I going to take only half the crops to market?

How will anyone believe my system of farming if/

OMAR: Aya. Come. Who could ever disbelieve you?

Even if they wanted to?

AYA laughs, girlish.

AYA: You…/

OMAR: *(Smiling, teasing.)* I'm not/

SEM: People are flooding in

How will we last til the spring?

AYA: Sem is right.

We have to make sure there is enough

The right foods being produced…

With pilfering/

OMAR: Look at this face…

Even with half a crop Sem
Would you believe she/

AYA: Flattery/

OMAR: Aya it's not/

AYA: Is an art…/

OMAR: Then let me continue…/

AYA: Oh no! No more./

She laughs some more, SEM joining in

OMAR: And why not?

Sem, do these cheeks look pink enough yet?

Aya, you're not even blushing yet

AYA: I am! Look/

Omar/

OMAR leans over and pinches AYA's cheeks. She giggles.

OMAR: *(Flattery.)* /Flattery is an art

Art needs a release

OMAR picks AYA up and tickles her. SEM joins in. They fall together in a heap. Finally SEM emerges, pulls up AYA (who is tough as a bird) and then they both pick up OMAR. Still laughing a little, they reassemble themselves at the table, AYA returning to her books.

OMAR: Aya, those boys only have their father…

AYA stops her calculations.

SEM: Soon they will be of marriageable age.

AYA: Someone needs to take them…

How do they survive?

SEM: The aunt is reluctant to take them on

AYA: Well. She has four husbands of her own already.

Running the dairy and taking care of six children…

It is no life.

AYA sighs.

AYA: OK fine, let them take the mangoes.

Let them have their taste for sweet things

OMAR: I'll talk to them tonight.

Perhaps we can give them some work around the orchard.

SEM: Some skills to make them more eligible.

AYA: Perhaps.

(Beat.)

Yes, we should.

AYA opens an envelope left on the table.

SEM: What is that?

AYA: The contract for the land in Mumbai

SEM stands close to her to read it.

SEM: You already have it?

AYA: Yes, these are the deeds.

The land will come into my name after the wedding

OMAR: And then you will go there?

AYA: Not for long my love

It will take maybe six months to establish the new community

SEM: It is a good time to expand Shaktipur

AYA: Yes, we have more people than ever

SEM: The last few conferences in Mumbai have excited many of the city people

AYA: We must engage them if we are to survive

AYA takes some money out and puts two equal piles on the table. It makes both men uncomfortable.

OMAR: We don't need that

AYA: No?

OMAR: What for? We have everything we need.

AYA: Maybe paper feels abstract where there is so much bounty around us.

But still this *paper*, can bring you the things you *want*.

Not need/

AYA makes both of them take the pile of money.

SEM: Aya we have everything we want

AYA: Choice. I'm giving you the chance to choose. Always.

AYA walks to the shrine and takes out a box. She opens ceremonially, waits until she has their attention, then raises it above her head and circling it three times clockwise. She then opens it. Inside are three gold chains and three special nuts.

AYA: And on this special day

A choice of another kind

One for each of my husbands, for what you give to me...

She takes one chain and places it around SEM's neck. She gives him a nut to eat.

AYA: For my first and sweetest love

For your kindness and warm heart

She kisses his forehead tenderly. He returns the affection, holding onto her. AYA releases him. She places the second chain carefully around OMAR's neck and then places the nut in his mouth.

AYA: For you darling Omar, for that gift to laugh, to love.

She strokes his chest slowly and looks into his eyes.

She walks to the middle of the table and places the last chain and nut back at the shrine.

AYA: I will go and get the flowers.

SEM: Yes Aya

Silence. AYA exits. OMAR drops a cup to the floor and watches it roll. SEM slumps against the worktop but continues chopping vegetables. OMAR stands and swoops the cup from the floor.

OMAR: Feed your husbands the fruits of last year's harvest.

A present to sweeten them against the sourest possibility...

SEM: Her belly is still flat.

Brother it is her *right*

OMAR exits. At the kitchen door he grabs the wheelbarrow and heads into the fields.

In the silence SEM pours the lentils into a pot on the stove.

SCENE 2: THE PAINTER

Mid-morning. Kitchen.

AYA is sitting on the floor. Basket of flowers on one side of her. She is preparing flowers for garlands.

SEM enters, and sits opposite her, taking a long thread and needle and measuring out the length of the garland. AYA puts the flowers on the floor between them and he threads them on.

SEM: Did you eat?

> *AYA shakes her head.*

SEM: I made you parota

AYA: I've lost my appetite.

SEM: You always eat breakfast…

AYA: I'm sorry, but I have no appetite today my love

SEM: Maybe it's the blood. It makes you sick?

AYA: You've always been so good at it.

> The fasting…
>
> I don't know how you do it

SEM: It's not difficult when you reap at the end…

> Like making love…

AYA: Yes…

> *Beat.*

SEM: We will make extra food as you suggested

> For the visitors from the 'outside'
>
> They can take some home

AYA: It will help

SEM: If people can find ways to feed themselves and their children

> They may think twice about killing/

AYA: The value of girls is more than just lack of food Sem

SEM: Yes.

> Still hungry stomachs can lead men to places they do not wish to go

AYA: Yes – make some extra, feed the outsiders
It may help them to see things differently

SEM: Shall I make you something?

AYA: No, Sem.
I am fine. Really

SEM: Such a big day. And no breakfast?

AYA: Still you do not sit still
Still like that small boy/

SEM: Aya/

AYA: It's a good thing.
(Beat.)
You're still young
Still have your boyish charms

SEM: Not so/

AYA: Young anymore?
I know, I know.
Forgive me.
When I look into your eyes
I see *everything* there
Memories from/

SEM: It was a long time ago/

AYA: You know what I mean Sem
Not like that
She grabs his hand and holds it tight.

AYA: Remember I held onto your hand before the wedding
ceremony?
The priestess was angry, for we were not even married
then!

SEM: I thought my blood would stop
And my hand would fall off
But when we finished, I realised it was not
My hand, but my heart that was gripped tightly

27

AYA: When I let go, you said
    Aya, please let go of my hand
    And I laughed because I already had

SEM: You were still holding on/

AYA: You were afraid

SEM: Not of you Aya
    Of/

AYA: Your feelings?
    Or maybe mine?
    (Beat.)
    It was a strange time
    After your brother's death

SEM: Something so sad and so happy at the same time
    A bit like today perhaps

SEM: Today is not a sad day Aya

AYA: In some ways, yes
    Others, no

SEM: I am happy Aya
    Perhaps this time
    A new husband
    Will mean a new family

AYA: Perhaps

SEM: You do your duty
    To this house
    To the community…

AYA: Yes. Still/
    (Beat.)
    You have always been here
    Given me what I need:
    A warm breeze on a cool night
    A cool breeze on a hot night

SEM: Yes. Always here Aya

    They have threaded a garland. SEM holds it up to AYA.

AYA: He will wear it well

When you have made it with such love

SEM: The colours blend well

AYA: They say some shades do not sit well together

But it is the way they are told to sit that is important

Is it not?

SEM laughs.

SEM: Do you talk of colours or husbands Aya?

AYA: Colours of course, dear husband

You are the artist – tell me

SEM gets up and begins tidying up a bit. Removing some paintings from the wall.

SEM: Colours can be blended

Even the most stubborn to

A purpose

A desire

But it is nature that is the real artist Aya

Not me… I always look to her

AYA: Nature has her way

We ours…

But when we have to take a detour

We have no choice but to continue walking

SEM: The wrong way?

AYA: Not wrong. Different

(Beat.)

Now, what happened with your paintings?

Did you submit them to the gallery?

SEM: Not yet Aya

AYA: Why not?

SEM: They're not ready.

We've been busy with/

AYA: You must never be too busy for your art

Food can wait.

SEM: Is that what I tell you when you come home?
    Hungry and tired?
    AYA laughs.

AYA: You must give me leftovers and say
    'Aya, I must feed my art first'
    I, will understand

SEM: Your hunger, like your mind, is not so easily distracted

AYA: Meaning?

SEM: *(Surrendering good naturedly.)* OK Aya!
    I will try next time
    But I know you
    You will walk to Mother's house

AYA: She likes me to eat there

SEM: And then you tell her your husbands…

AYA: *(Smiling.)* /Didn't take care of me?
    I wouldn't

SEM: Your presence there is enough…
    To say everything

AYA: You think she doesn't know what you do?

SEM: It is never enough

AYA: Oh Sem
    Mother/ everyone knows what you do
    You are enough
    Always. Enough
    Beat. SEM continues packing his paintings away.

SEM: Omar says if it was enough/

AYA: /Yes, Omar
    He is still young in our world
    (Beat.)
    You know I do not expect you to stop painting

SEM: It is a pastime Aya

AYA: You're talented
    Submit your paintings to the gallery in Mumbai next
    month

SEM: It's not what I want

    Besides, what will everyone say?

AYA: I don't expect you to sacrifice your talent

SEM: Isn't that what marriage is?

    Sacrifice?

AYA: Compromise

    But not all of yourself

SEM: Pure love does not ask of the other

    But simply the pleasure of giving

    I am not sacrificing

    I am content

AYA: Why do you take them (the paintings) off the wall?

SEM: The Fiancé.

    Your Fiancé.

    The trousseau will arrive this afternoon

    We must make space

    For him

    And his belongings

AYA: *(Silencing SEM.)* Space?!

    He will fit in, find his own space.

SEM: You do not understand men as I do

    AYA laughs, and takes a painting from SEM's hand and puts it back on the wall.

AYA: Perhaps not

    Still, your paintings will stay

    Everything will stay

SEM: Change is a good thing sometimes Aya

    Even if we do not want it

AYA: You mean that?

SEM: Of course. Your plans are bigger than me

    Bigger than just this house

    (Beat.)

    I know you want a child more than anyone

Tender, AYA kisses SEM. It is a kiss of affection not passion – beautiful and sincere.

AYA: Sem, you would not mind if you did not do the sacrifice?

SEM: *(Hurt, surprised.)* You do not want me to?

AYA: There's no need my darling

SEM: But Aya, she knows me

AYA: *(Snapping.)* It's bad enough isn't it? Without you wanting to watch!

SEM: *(Taken aback, eyes lowered.)* You said/

AYA: *(Recovering composure.)* No.
This is one thing I can not
Let you do

SEM: It will be better for her

AYA: And you?
Do you not think of yourself?

SEM: There perhaps something of myself too

AYA: To see something you nursed, killed?

SEM: To send her in peace

AYA: Omar will be kind

SEM: But not loving

AYA: When you cook the lamb
Cook it with love

SEM: Forgive me Aya
But I think you think of Omar before the lamb

AYA: Perhaps… He is a little wounded

SEM: We knew about the engagement months ago/

AYA: Knowing and the reality are different things
He needs extra care today

SEM: So you bestow him the privilege?
Out of pity?

AYA: I think of both of you
Never just one

AYA puts her finger to her lips. She pulls out her SACRED BOTTLE filled with menstrual blood.

AYA: A woman's blood is the best protection a man can have

You need not worry about anything Sem

SEM lowers his head to allow her to dab it on the back of his neck. She kisses his forehead, holds on to him.

SCENE 3: THE FISHERMAN

Late morning. Kitchen. AYA on the floor again, preparing flowers for the second garland. OMAR enters carrying dirty bed sheets and personal items (books, clothing.) from AYA's bedroom.

AYA: Why are you doing that?

OMAR: Why not?

AYA: It is not your job

OMAR: I need these things

AYA: Come sit

She pats the space next to her.

OMAR: I want to take these to *my* room

AYA: Later. Come, sit.

He drops the sheets on the floor. On top lie some of his personal effects – a book, some clothing. He sits down. She rubs his back.

AYA: You can leave your belongings in my room

OMAR: I prefer to take them

AYA: As you wish

But you will find them back there soon enough

OMAR: You will need space for your new husband will you not?

AYA: I did not ask you to move them

(Beat.)

OMAR: Perhaps I will take them to the coast

AYA: When?

OMAR: *(Little afraid.)* When I next go

AYA returns to her task. Refusing to react to OMAR's threat.

AYA: You know garland making is the job of the husbands

OMAR: Then let me

AYA: No. I'll do it.

> For you…

AYA continues with the garlands.

AYA: I want them to be heavy

OMAR: You have enough

AYA finds one last flower.

OMAR: The thread will break

AYA threads its on.

AYA: Are you so sure?

OMAR: Maybe not now

> But at the ceremony

AYA adds the last one, smiling at OMAR. Cajoling him almost, to disagree. The garland is complete.

AYA: A garland should be like a chain of gold

> Looking light

> But feels heavy

She fingers OMAR's chain.

AYA: I thought this one would suit you best

OMAR: I thought it was Mother who chose them

AYA: It should have been Mother

> But I told her

> If I have to see them everyday, then

> Surely it is for me to choose

OMAR: Like your husbands?

> …

> Like your *new* husband?

AYA laughs.

AYA: Come my love.

She stands and takes the SACRED BOTTLE from her pocket and dabs the blood on his neck. As she does so, he takes a kiss from her, she does not object, but does not fully engage either.

OMAR: You feel I always want too much, but I wish simply to feel your heart.

AYA: *(Laughing.)* My heart?

OMAR: Last night as you lay there, coated in the sweat of pleasure
You turned your back on me

AYA: *(Surprised.)* What does that mean Omar?
If I turn toward or away from you –
After the fact?
That I love you less?

OMAR: You never used to do that

AYA: *(Weary.)* I was tired

OMAR: You were *tired?*

AYA: Well, yes…
Pleasure is exhausting sometimes

OMAR: So now you complain of that also?

AYA: I do not complain
I state fact…
I was tired

OMAR: So you turned away?

AYA: So I went to sleep

OMAR: And today?

AYA: Today I am not tired
Yet

OMAR: And tonight you bring someone else to your bed

AYA: This is *the way*

OMAR: This wasn't *our* way

AYA: This is the way
The way it's always been….
You've always known that

OMAR: *(Shaking head, voice low.)* No…!
I knew you were a grieving widow.
Your first husband dead.
His brother in a separate bed!

AYA reaches out to him and caresses him.

OMAR: You have energy for everything.
Shaktipur, the land, even trips to the city
But not us
Not anymore…

AYA: *(Frustrated.)* Again?!

OMAR: When we make love you close your eyes
It's as if your mind is somewhere else
Rummaging through old memories or finding new
possibilities
Anywhere but with me

AYA: We are together as often as we used to…

OMAR: Your body is there, but your heart is not Aya…
You do not talk to me as you used to…
Why is it always up to me to entice you?
Do you think it's only this *(Touching her.)* that I want?
That I don't *feel* anything?

AYA: Of course I know
But you're always demanding something Omar…
Always wanting more…

OMAR: And why shouldn't I? You're my wife!

AYA: Why do you say that?
'Your wife', your belonging…

OMAR: How could you understand Aya?
I am but one star in the sky to you
But to me, you are the silver moon
AYA smiles, sad.

OMAR: You've closed yourself to me
I can feel it…

AYA creates physical distance between them. Upset.

OMAR: *(Quiet, almost to self.)* You think I can't do it.
That I am cold and infertile
But I am not Aya. *I am not*

AYA is not able to look at him.

AYA: *(Whispering.)* I know.

> *(Beat.)*

> But what can I do?

OMAR: *(Shaking his head.)* I can not…

> Can not Aya.

AYA: You can!

> We can endure this

> You/We have to

> *AYA wraps her arms around his shoulders.*

AYA: Remember when your mother found us in the boat that night?

OMAR: Of course

AYA: She said that she didn't know how an old woman like me could move like that!

OMAR: You *liked* to make it rock…

AYA: *(Smiling.)* Maybe…

OMAR: Remember the water used to come in and soak the bottom?

> You didn't care…

AYA: I did. Just not as much as you

OMAR: The noise used to wake the neighbours…

AYA: It was embarrassing

> Sometimes

> *(Beat.)*

OMAR: And now you want me to listen to you and him?

> *OMAR turning to face her, pushing her hands away.*

> I do not know what you want of me Aya.

> Am I your friend, your lover, your confidante?

AYA: *(Sighing.)* I told you once

> Love is a meal.

> You can not have one dish without the other.

OMAR: You'll never understand…

AYA: I understand you loved your boat.

    Loved it as much as your mother hated me

OMAR: Is that why you asked me to give it all up?

    My life outside this place?

    My freedom?

AYA: *(Slightly defiant.)* Yes

OMAR: *(Quietly flattered.)* She doesn't hate you

    She's a mother

    She wants grandchildren…

AYA: Like all mothers.

    Once is not enough

    They want everyone to do it!

    (Beat.)

OMAR: Does he make you happy Aya?

    Happier than me?

AYA: *(Genuine.)* No.

    I still love you the same.

OMAR: But you still bring him

    To give you a child?

    (Beat.)

AYA: *No, no.*

    For the community

    For all of this!

OMAR: *(Frustrated.)* To give you what I can not!

AYA: *(Softer, coming closer to him.)* I want you…

    AYA tries to kiss him. OMAR resists.

OMAR: Don't touch me…

AYA: I don't want this to change us

    Change the way you make me feel alive

    Feel free…

OMAR: So free you can…/

AYA: /Shhhh… I want to protect this as much as you.

    (Beat.)

Believe me, when I say

It is not about a child

Can you understand there are parts of a room

That remain undiscovered?

OMAR: And me?

Do you think you know me so well?

AYA: I know it is not fair…

But I try my best to let you have your freedoms

OMAR: But I do not want those freedoms Aya!

AYA: Perhaps not now

But/

(Beat.)

We will be together always.

OMAR lets her take his hand.

AYA: My love, whether there is another husband or not

I promise you *if* I have a child it will be yours

OMAR: And the others?

AYA: I promise.

It will be yours

He grasps her hand tighter. AYA caresses him, but physically seeking reassurance at the same time, perhaps wrapping OMAR's arms around her.

OMAR: You mean that?

This is not just about the bedroom Aya

They kiss, long and hard. AYA laughs.

AYA: *(Laughing a little.)* No, not about just the bedroom

OMAR pushes AYA down and unwrapping her clothes.

OMAR: Shhh.

AYA: I surrender

OMAR: I didn't ask you to

AYA: No?

She undresses him.

Then, just a taste. A small taste

He resists a little

OMAR: You can never have just a taste, my love

AYA: You will always be here

She touches her heart. He smiles.

AYA unwraps her sari. He sits her down in front of him and plays a finger up and down her spine, she sighs in pleasure.

AYA: I still need you…

OMAR holds her close, clearly roused.

AYA: *(Softer.)* Want you…

OMAR moves his hands to her lower back and then begins kissing her neck.

AYA: We will go *together*

To your boat

Make it move again

SCENE 4: THE ARRIVAL

Some time later: Kitchen.

OMAR and SEM struggling with cooking which is almost done. They pour the food into ornate pots which line the table.

SEM: The onions are sticking

OMAR: Add some water

SEM: You didn't close the lid enough

SEM adds some more water.

SEM: They needs to absorb the flavor… But not burn

OMAR: Brother, I'm sorry, my mind is distracted

…

The last wedding, it was just you

Who did all of this

SEM: Now there are two of us

It is better

OMAR: Does it get easier?

SEM: *Ease* is not the word I would use

OMAR: This is what you told me once

Now I see what you mean brother

SEM puts his hand on OMAR's arm to reassure him. Then attends to the onions on the stove.

SEM: Can you smell the cardamom?

OMAR: Cinnamon as well

My mouth is watering brother!

SEM: *(Rueful.)* Some things will never change…

OMAR: *(Smiling a little.)* Fasting and cooking do not make a good marriage

SEM: Sometimes marriage of the unlikely creates better friends than lovers

SEM finishes with the onions.

SEM: *(Embarrassed.)* You know, I couldn't…

We couldn't

OMAR: It's not your fault brother

It is Aya who does not know what she really wants

Knock on the door. The men are surprised.

SEM: Perhaps another baby?

OMAR: None are due until next month

SEM: No one would have business with Aya today

…

I'll go

SEM goes to open it. JEROME stands there, he is dressed up as if for a wedding. He carries a large wrapped gift in both hands.

JEROME: Hello?

SEM: Namaskar.

JEROME places the gift on the floor and then attempts a semblance of a Namaskar. Failing.

SEM: Can we help you?

JEROME: Oh yes… Well, I'm Professor Edwards, from London

SEM: Yes?

JEROME picks up the gift and shows it to SEM.

JEROME: I've brought a gift. For the wedding

OMAR: A gift?

JEROME: Do you take gifts?

    I'm sorry if I…

    It's just so/

SEM: *(Faintly amused.)* / Hot?

    Yes, come

    Come in.

    JEROME enters, looks around surprised. OMAR greets him.

JEROME: It's different to what I expected.

    I'm sorry, I'm Professor. Edwards

    Agriculture; Research Fellow, University College London.

SEM: I'm Sem and this is Omar.

    SEM takes the gift.

SEM: Thank you – for this

    Aya will/

OMAR: Your shoes?

JEROME: Oh yes, sorry

    I didn't think

OMAR: Your shoes…

    JEROME reluctantly takes off his sandals and leaves them by the door. He seats himself. SEM gives him the water. JEROME drinks with relish.

    OMAR picks up the gift, examines it suspiciously.

SEM: It is very hot now

    Not a time to be outside

JEROME: Feels like rain though, don't you think?

SEM: There is no rain this time of year

JEROME: Some sort of closeness in the atmosphere

    Pressure changes, my head is always the first to feel it

    Migraines…

SEM: Perhaps the heat…/

OMAR: It never rains on the festival day

SEM: Aya says in all her life it has always been the same
One endlessly long day, with the sun beating down
Rain today would be a bad omen...
Aya says/

JEROME: Yes, Aya...
Where is she?

(Beat.)

OMAR: The wedding is not until evening Professor

SEM: /But of course, you are welcome to rest in the meantime

JEROME: The evening?
Well I have plenty of time

OMAR: Do you have business with her?

JEROME: No...

OMAR: Good, because today there is no business

JEROME: Of course. Today is the festival
I know Aya, you see
Perhaps she mentioned me?

OMAR: Never

SEM: You know Aya from the conferences in the city?

JEROME: Yes – our research overlaps
I've been studying Indian agricultural techniques for many
years now
So we are often at the same place at the same time
...
Last year she gave that fantastic speech. With a standing
ovation too
Passionate isn't she?

OMAR: For a woman?

JEROME: No for a person who/
Well never mind

OMAR: *(Sarcastic.)* Everyone is educated *here Sahib*

JEROME: Of course, I know you're all educated

OMAR: *(Sarcastic.)* Of course

SEM: Thank you for the gift

JEROME: I thought gift giving was the least I could do

    Is Aya around perhaps?

SEM: You know a little of our community?

JEROME: They speak of you all across India: this Shaktipur

    This village… Community

    Some say it's a cult

    Others, Women

    Save all their earnings to come here

    They say it is a blessed place. A type of utopia

OMAR: We do good here…

SEM: Years ago no one could grow rice here, too dry they said.

    Now look at the paddies!

    There was no grass to graze the animals, no fish in the river.

    Now there is not one empty stomach here!

    The Goddess watches over us…

    Blesses Aya with fingers

    Of fertility.

    She can grow anything

JEROME: Yes. Many are eager to learn of her techniques

OMAR: We can give Aya the gift

SEM: It is very hot outside

    You can rest here doctor

JEROME: Very kind of you Sem

    Indians are known for their hospitality

OMAR: For good reason

JEROME: Is the bride always kept hidden away?

OMAR: She is not hidden

JEROME: Could you ask her if I could see her?

OMAR: Why? Is it urgent?

JEROME: I'd like to give her the gift – personally

    As is the custom

OMAR: *Your* custom

SEM: Professor, Aya is not in the house

She is outside checking on the animals

JEROME: Oh I see

Why didn't you say?

Both men ignore him.

JEROME: I suppose you are not used to foreigners here?

SEM: Professor, many foreigners come to find out about Aya's farming 'techniques'

OMAR: The last time, they wanted to buy the patent

JEROME: That would be natural

But I can assure you I'm not here for that

OMAR: It is *natural* that the technique stays with her

With us, *here*

JEROME: But how will you help the others?

The people outside your community?

SEM: Tonight we invite everyone to feast with us

JEROME: And stay if they wish?

SEM: Yes. Anyone who wishes to take up our way of life is accepted

OMAR: Except foreigners

JEROME: And those that do not accept your way of life?

You keep these farming concepts to yourselves?

You keep them locked away in this remote place?

OMAR: They are not secrets

SEM: They, like our way of life, can only be understood

By living them

JEROME: So sharing your success with others is not your priority?

OMAR: Our priority is to succeed here

There is no way to 'succeed' out there

JEROME: And you protect it well I see…

I suppose you think you need the guards too?

OMAR: To prevent outsiders

JEROME: *(Laughing.)* Outsiders?

OMAR: /from causing mischief

SEM: Things are bad outside
>Last week a fourteen-year-old girl was murdered
>For refusing to marry into a family of four brothers

OMAR: Set alight... By her parents

SEM: Outside, people are desperate
>If the rest of India could see how we live here
>Surely things would change
>Before the guards, every so often a woman would be abducted

JEROME: They only want them for marriage
>To create children?

SEM: Yes

JEROME: What a paradox: The denigrated sex
>Is the most desired at the same time

SEM: Girls cost their family money;
>A dowry is expensive
>Families must pay someone to marry their daughters

OMAR: The outside does not value women

JEROME: In England we have too many unattached women
>Highly educated, but no man in sight
>Funny that paradox

SEM: *(Eager.)* But we are expanding...

JEROME: So I heard

>*OMAR distances himself. SEM and OMAR return to their cooking.*
>*JEROME studies the room and watches SEM.*

JEROME: So you do all the cooking in here?
>For everyone?

SEM: Everyone brings food for the festival
>But we provide the most tonight
>Because it is also Aya's wedding...

JEROME: You have no servants?

    No house boys or girls?

SEM: Generally yes. But they have a day to spend with their families

JEROME: Why do they call it the Night of the Flowers?

SEM: Flowers are the plant's sexual organs

    They are beautiful to entice

    Nature has her ways

    Calling on insects to do their work

    But those bees are male…

    They work only for the Queen

    JEROME laughs.

JEROME: I'm sorry. Maybe if you could explain what it is a celebration of?

SEM: A celebration of the harvest

    As the new moon rises, the air fills with the scent of flowers

    We give thanks to the Goddess Kali tonight.

    Prayers at sundown and then dancing until dawn

    The air will be filled with pollen, seeds adrift in the wind

OMAR: Everything that *could be*…

    Will be…

JEROME: Kali, the demon Goddess

SEM: You misunderstand

OMAR: *Again*

SEM: That which is born must be destroyed

    and that which is destroyed must be born again…

    It is the cycle that keeps the world turning

    One can not be without the other…

JEROME: So a celebration of life, of birth.

    I can't argue with that.

    Not here or all places, can I?

    OMAR adds tomatoes to the onions. Sizzling. He adds some chilli. The air burns.

JEROME: *(Coughing.)* And the bedrooms? You have one each?

> *SEM nods. Closing the lid on the pan and giving OMAR a warning look.*

OMAR: *(Sarcastic.)* Perhaps you would like a guided tour Professor Edwards?

JEROME: It's just so amazing to see this all in action

I've heard so much about it from Aya

OMAR: *(Suspicious.)* Aya lectures on horticultural techniques not/

JEROME: *(Smiling, caught out.)* Of course, but its impossible to separate the woman from her way of life.

…

I see you wear no marital bands? The anklets I mean.

SEM: Aya doesn't believe in them

JEROME: She's a bit of a rebel isn't she?

OMAR: We are not prisoners or commodities

JEROME: Your words, or your wife's?

> *OMAR smoulders. Silence.*

OMAR: This is Aya's way. The life I choose to lead

JEROME: So you were not born here?

SEM: Omar came as a young man.

His mother lives in the village with her two husbands.

JEROME: And your father?

OMAR: He lives at the coast.

JEROME: But you stayed here?

OMAR: Of course.

JEROME: And your mother? Any girls?

> *OMAR shakes his head.*

JEROME: And you?

SEM: I was born into this…

JEROME: You are Aya's first husband?

SEM: No. She married my brother.

After he died she took me

JEROME: As simple as that?

SEM: It is the way

JEROME: She must have been quite beautiful when you married her

SEM: She still is

JEROME: Yes. Indeed.

SEM: Lust clouds but

Love enlightens the subconscious

JEROME: *(Not understanding at all.)* Yes

…

So where are all the animals?

SEM: Sleeping in the barns.

They rest during the afternoon

JEROME: Makes sense to me

OMAR: *(Sarcastic.)* Things appear to make sense when you look from the outside

JEROME ignores him.

JEROME: Some might say that this way of life is animalistic

SEM laughs.

SEM: Only if you were very foolish

JEROME: They; animals, show the truth, cut back and exposed, without our sentimentalities

(Beat.)

JEROME reaches for a piece of fruit.

JEROME: Do you mind?

SEM: You can't eat that…

OMAR: We fast today.

No food, only water…

JEROME: Well I'm Anglican

OMAR: Well, here you're nothing

JEROME: What's that supposed to mean?

SEM: Here your religion must be left at the door

JEROME: *(To SEM.)* So I must fast too?

SEM: Of course. All the men fast for the Kali puja.

> *(Beat.)*

JEROME: If you insist…

> *JEROME slowly puts the fruit down.*
>
> *AYA enters carrying some flowers; she is startled to see JEROME but conceals it.*

JEROME: *(Bowing.)* Aya

AYA: *(Shocked, but immaculately hiding it.)* Professor Edwards?
> *Welcome.* How are you?

> *SEM picks up the gift and hands it to AYA. She barely looks at it before placing it on the table.*

SEM: He has brought a gift

AYA: A gift? You didn't need to go to so much trouble

OMAR: *(Accusing.)* He's come for the wedding

AYA: My love, *(Both men look.)* this is Jerome.
> Remember I spoke of him?
> He's helped me get some papers published in the UK
> *(Faintly confrontational.)*
> So you've come

JEROME: I have…
> You see, I would not miss this, for the world
> Seeing you take *another* husband
> I've read so much about them

AYA: *(Laughing.)* My husbands?

JEROME: No…
> I admit, I have an ulterior motive
> I'm writing a paper and thought I'd pay you a visit

AYA: So this is not a social call?

JEROME: Research and pleasure go well together wouldn't you agree?

AYA: Professor Edwards, as you can see – today I am otherwise engaged

If it is an urgent research question, Sem and Omar can take you round

JEROME: Your methods of irrigation and farming are so unusual…

I believe only you would be able to provide *answers*

AYA: I don't believe it could be anything pressing could it?

JEROME: Indeed it is I'm afraid

I have some *urgent queries*

I could ask *the husbands*

But I doubt they could help me

AYA looks at JEROME as if weighing him up. She sits down, giving in.

OMAR: I told him Aya

That this was not something he could just learn

JEROME: 'Very effective', says the research, 'revolutionary' I've been told

AYA: Yes. Effective.

Revolutionary? Not when it's existed for hundreds of years

JEROME: But you have re-invigorated it…

AYA: Let's leave it as effective

OMAR: And '*ours*'

(Beat.)

It can not be given so freely

JEROME: The literature says women here have an almanac-like knowledge of plant varieties

AYA: Such big words for something so simple, professor

JEROME: Outside of Shakitpur, they say the knowledge of the plants; horticulture is dying out, without the women. Women like you

OMAR: Perhaps Professor Edwards would like to rest at your Mother's house?

There is more space there

More husbands for you to meet

For your *research*

JEROME: My research is horticultural.

Besides, I wouldn't want to impose

51

SEM: He is our guest Aya
How would it look if/

JEROME: I don't mind staying here and observing
Or even helping out…

SEM: Forgive us professor. We are not used to observers

JEROME: If Aya would just grant me a moment of her time

OMAR: I told him.
There is no business today!
Aya we must prepare for the sacrifice

AYA: Yes. Of course my love…

AYA finds the garlands covered in a towel. The smell is overpowering.

AYA: Tell me… Do you have flowers like this in the west?

JEROME: No… But we have others just as sweet

AYA: I doubt that…

JEROME: Some would say flowers are flowers
Full of colour and scent

AYA: Some say men are men:
Full of brawn and little sense

JEROME: You're being a little harsh.

OMAR: Excuse me. We must continue with the preparations
Aya

OMAR asks JEROME to move out of the way so he can carry on his work. Throughout the rest of the scene, JEROME presents himself as a physical obstacle to the wedding preparations.

JEROME: So what will you wear?
Something white
Something borrowed, or something blue?

AYA: Not a dress
But white, yes

JEROME: The colour of virgins

AYA laughs. OMAR moves JEROME's bag out of the way. JEROME puts it on the table.

SEM: Here white, red and gold

> White for purity
> Gold for wealth

OMAR: Red for fertility

JEROME: Your fertility counts for so much

OMAR: Surely no different in your land?

JEROME: Women in the west do not *have* to have children...

OMAR: *(Sarcastic.)* Really? Are there many childless women?

JEROME: No…

> Presumably they have made their choice
> To have children

OMAR: *(Sarcastic.)* Obviously...

JEROME: They can *choose*

> Not to have children,
> But most *choose* to have them

SEM: *(Cutting in.)*

> Here a woman's greatest gift is having a child
> That is why we worship her
> There is nothing wrong with that

> *OMAR moves JEROME's bag, he objects, but seeing OMAR's face – relents*

JEROME: *(Watching OMAR.)* Of course not.

> *OMAR dumps the bag outside the kitchen.*

AYA: Perhaps some fresh lime and water

> Omar can you bring some?

OMAR: In a moment

AYA: As soon as you can my love

> *(Beat.)*

> But even in 'your land', of 'choice'
> Women, are they as free as us?

JEROME: Perhaps not

> Less power and more expectations on them
> Less boundaries as well

AYA: We have boundaries too

> Customs that make life easier here

JEROME: Like?

SEM: They are subtle.

> For instance, a man can not see his child being born.

AYA: *(Laughing.)* No woman wants a man to see her give birth!

JEROME: You do not know this

AYA: Did you see your children being born?

JEROME: You assume I have children…

> *OMAR brings the lime juice. JEROME takes a sip, it is sour. Very sour.*

AYA: What's wrong?

JEROME: It's very tart

AYA: Sour?

> *AYA admonishes OMAR. Getting up and adding sugar syrup herself.*
> *She indicates to JEROME's wedding ring*

AYA: *(Knowing the answer.)* You are married Professor Edwards?

JEROME: *(Conceding.)* Was. Yes

AYA: *(Surprise.)* You *were* married?

> How can you no longer be married?

JEROME: Yes. We dissolved our marriage

AYA: *(Mirth.)* Like sugar in tea?

> Where did you dissolve it?

JEROME: In the courts

AYA: You realize, that love can not be dissolved

> Into thin air
> Once created it must evolve into something
> Else

JEROME: Friendship perhaps?

> You speak of all relationships?
> Not just marriage

AYA: Yes

> And the rest?
> Where did the rest of the feelings go?

JEROME: I still love my wife.

In some ways I suppose…

AYA: Of course you do.

And the children?

JEROME: They are too old to care anymore about the state of their parent's marriage

AYA: They had cause to worry

The parent's quarrels always splinter a child's heart

…

Perhaps you forgot how to understand your wife – as a woman

JEROME: *(Changing the subject.)* Perhaps

Perhaps, this is as you say – the strength of this place

Your Shaktipur

(Beat.)

Even the air feels different

It breeds something…

AYA: Girls.

JEROME: What?

AYA: Here we breed and protect our girls from what is outside.

From deaths so dark I wonder who could conceive them;

Opium in milk, drowning in wells, death by sand burial

And now even though they have made it illegal

They still whisk away those baby girls with machines

The government pretends not to see…

To see would be to admit defeat

So they prefer blind and deaf

Like the mauled children

Begging for money for self-inflicted ailments

(Beat.)

But our girls; they are born to smiles and their lips brought to their mother's breast before even their first cry…

See how we cherish them.

So *Jerome,* yes, in a sense, we breed...

JEROME: It was so strange to see so many of them.
Running, giggling.
At the coast I saw only a handful
I hear the clinics in Mumbai are filled
The old practices transformed
To modern day murders
Yet, here you have plenty...

AYA: *(Sigh.)* Hundreds
And yet, we still don't have enough...
So we carry on
Breeding.

JEROME: It is wonderful.
This tranquility, free thinking and .../

AYA: So you are wide-eyed and full of awe?

JEROME: Awed yes. The first thing I saw were two sisters
walking with six husbands in tow...

AYA: *(Knowing.)* Then you are not so awed.
Already you *(Meaning all of them.)* feel insecure

JEROME: Insecure?

AYA: *(Smiling, but condescending.)* So intelligent,
But still you can not fail to act on your indignation!

JEROME: Perhaps

AYA: If you look beyond your fear
You will see that here we teach how it is to love
Without possession...
'love is about surrender not fear.'
(Beat.)

AYA: Boys or girls?

JEROME: What?

AYA: Your children
Boys or girls?

JEROME: Two girls

AYA: So you are blessed

JEROME: Yes. And this, this is like a parental love

AYA: No, you misunderstand…

If you're always doubting, all you'll see is doubt

JEROME: Science is doubt first, think later

AYA: So it is not knowledge that propels you, but uncertainty
Still, you are here now…

(Smiling.)

You should stay and learn what it's all about
For *yourself*

(Beat.)

JEROME: … But

AYA: We will talk about your questions later
Take some rest
Have no doubt, I will find you

SCENE 5: THE LOVER

Sometime later. Bedroom. AYA is in the bath.

JEROME watches her from the bed. On the side is the gift he has brought. She examines her breasts and stomach and then gets out, wrapping the towel around herself.

She is startled when she sees JEROME. They stare at each other; JEROME comes forward to kiss her. AYA responds and then pulls away.

AYA: Jerome, it's not the best time

JEROME: I would have come sooner, *if* you told me of the wedding

AYA: I knew you wouldn't approve

JEROME: I suppose I knew this was a bad idea.

(Beat.)

But I couldn't stop myself.

AYA: Shame.

(Beat.)

Some emotions cling like bush ants.

But we must learn to live with them.

Not act on them

JEROME: You said/

AYA: Now I am Leader

Not a follower

(Beat.)

AYA: *(Softly.)* What happened with your wife?

JEROME: We had our differences…

AYA: Here we don't cast fish back into the ocean

JEROME: She wanted her freedom

She noticed I had already taken mine

AYA: She was angry

JEROME: I told her it wasn't that I had taken mine

Rather you had taken it from me

AYA: I didn't take anything from you

That you did not want to give

(Beat.)

JEROME: Why didn't you call me?

Before you set your heart on this marriage?

On this 'plan' you have Aya?

AYA: Why?

JEROME: I told you if you were in trouble to find me

AYA: That's your trouble Jerome

You expect *trouble*

JEROME: You seem so free when we are together

But in this place it seems, you are a different person.

AYA: Not different. Real

We share some moments

They are sweet, like the morning breeze

But the day must go on…

JEROME: So that's it?

AYA: *(Smiling a little, despite herself.)* The tender, cool caress of
a breeze

JEROME: So that's why you never called?
　　Why you were pleased each time a
　　conference was over?

AYA: Not pleased. It was just the nature of things.
　　We always stay together until the last day
　　You go home and so do I.

JEROME: Then you forgot me like an old chair?

AYA: I don't forget
　　I wait until next time we are together
　　…
　　What is it you wanted me to do?

JEROME: I just thought – you would have given me the
　　opportunity to/

AYA: What?

JEROME: Present myself

AYA: As you know, the reasons for marriage are complex

JEROME: *(Eager.)* Are they *forcing you*?

AYA: *No*
　　I want to take Shaktipur to the city
　　Bring the teachings to the urban people
　　Teach them what they have lost
　　Create change from the rich to the poor

JEROME: So you marry for *politics?*

AYA: I marry a man who believes in me, in this
　　He has land in Mumbai for Shaktipur
　　We will go there and create a new community

JEROME: And then what? Then they will all become breeding
　　grounds?
　　Honestly Aya, what you're creating is something medieval
　　Something taking women back to old times /

AYA: Medieval?!
　　During the times your people were burning women as
　　witches, ours were leading communities!

JEROME: You still kill girls and burn women. Tell me if sati is
    extinct

AYA: *Outside.* Here no woman will ever be burnt or subjugated
    You might criticize; think I can do nothing against the
    masses
    But we have proven this works
    We have more girls than ever before

JEROME: Ah! There you are, *my Aya*
    Still that passion burning in the core of your body
    So strong, independent
    Yet why do abide by these 'traditions'?

AYA: You can laugh if you like
    But this is my decision

JEROME: You're making a mistake Aya
    They're using you!

AYA: You don't believe I want this man?
    That this is a choice of my own?
    From my heart and loins?

JEROME: Don't Aya.
    You sound/

AYA: What?

JEROME: Crude

    AYA laughs.

JEROME: You laugh at an old man like me
    Because you haven't yet lived

AYA: *(Gentle.)* But I have
    I have lived *here*
    In *my world*, not yours
    Silence.

JEROME: So you do not need me

AYA: I will always need you…

JEROME: And the others? Your Husbands/

AYA: Them also

JEROME: I can't understand this place

AYA: You understand love

So you understand Shaktipur

JEROME: Perhaps this was a little rash

You are right, I don't belong here

I should go…

AYA: Thank you for the gift

Perhaps you should take it back with you.

JEROME picks up the gift and knocks over the bowl and knife. Blood pours down onto the floor.

AYA: Let me

JEROME is too fast and picks up the two items.

JEROME: What is this?

AYA: Leave it

She tries to take the knife and bowl back.

JEROME: So much blood

AYA: It's nothing

JEROME: Are you ill?

AYA: No

Jerome, *please*

JEROME: Then why?

AYA: It's better if you do not know

JEROME: Why do you say that my darling?

If there is something wrong…

Tell me

AYA: It's for the menstrual blood…

A custom: see?

She shows JEROME the SACRED BOTTLE, and pours the blood from the bowl into it.

AYA: When Shaktipur's women marry, we present the bottle as proof of fertility and empty womb

A woman who is pregnant can not marry until the child is over three years

JEROME: Seems an arbitrary figure

AYA: Perhaps. But both child and mother are somewhat independent by then. A new marriage would not endanger the welfare of the infant

JEROME smiles at AYA.

JEROME: But, this is a lot of blood…

AYA: Each month we fill it with menstrual blood
And dab it onto the neck of our men
For protection

JEROME: *(Recoiling slightly.)* They *let* you do that?

AYA: *(Smiling.)* They *want* me to do it
A blessing not to be given lightly

AYA opens the bottle and dabs her finger with the blood.

AYA: It is only for the husbands

JEROME cringes, but AYA's fingers caress the back of his neck tenderly.

AYA: Jerome
You have listened to my dreams, nurtured me, *made* love to me
Come…

JEROME lets AYA dab the back of his neck. He is almost timid, but at the same time – incredulous. AYA is gentle. She kisses him.

JEROME: Too much for one woman
So tell me, what is my beautiful Aya doing with a knife and a bowl of blood?

AYA: I told you

AYA takes the bowl and knife from JEROME.

JEROME: Yes
You have told me a truth
But not a fact

AYA: I've told you what it's for

JEROME: And the knife?

> *AYA turns away from him.*
>
> You state facts, yes:
> You have blood – for your sacred bottle
> Proof of your fertility and empty womb
> Your ticket to marriage and your new husband
> *(Beat.)*
> But it is not your blood is it?

AYA: It is *mine*

JEROME: *Yours?* Like everything in this house
> Including your husbands are yours?
> But it did not come from you
> Did it Aya?

AYA: It is mine

JEROME: You are not a good liar

AYA: I am not lying

JEROME: You tell a half truth like a fact!

AYA: Leave it Jerome!

JEROME: No, not until you tell me
> *(Beat.)*
> You want to tell me Aya
> Don't you?

AYA: I have nothing to say!

JEROME: Tell me now Aya, or should I ask Sem?

AYA: No Jerome. Stop

JEROME: Perhaps he would know where or why you have this?

AYA: Please!

JEROME: All you have to do is tell the truth

AYA: It is not mine

JEROME: That I know

Where did you get the blood Aya?

AYA: From the lamb

JEROME: What lamb?

He wipes the back of his neck.

AYA: The sacrificial lamb

For tonight

JEROME: Really?

AYA: Yes. Why not?

She will die anyway

JEROME: *(Incredulous but slightly in awe.)* Oh Aya…

AYA: Stop saying that.

JEROME: When did you? Find out I mean?

She ignores him, but is shaking.

JEROME: When Aya?!

AYA: … A few days ago

JEROME: So my Aya is with child

(Beat.)

AYA: Yes

JEROME: *Oh Aya. My sweet, sweet Aya*

AYA: Stop it

JEROME: I thought you said you couldn't have any?

JEROME gets up, pacing. Thinking.

AYA: Apparently I was wrong

JEROME: Are you sure?

AYA: Yes

JEROME: And now, you just marry again

Against your 'customs'?

What you so believe in?

AYA: I believe in the practice of equality

I never said I believed in this

Nobody asked me if I wanted a child!

JEROME: They will never let you

AYA: They don't need to know

JEROME: But you can't lie to them surely

AYA: You won't tell them

JEROME: Aya, how can I sit back and let you do this?

AYA: Promise not to say a word

JEROME: This won't work Aya. Your little plan
Even if you marry this man… They'll find out in the end

AYA: No. I'll go to Mumbai after the wedding

JEROME: Abort the child and do the very thing you/

AYA: I was never against *choice* Jerome…
You know that

JEROME: Ha! The Leader who breaks all the rules
You people have a habit of doing that…

AYA: *(Resisting the urge to slap him.)* Which people?
She drops. Stares at JEROME.

AYA: The person you say you love?

JEROME: Forgive me Aya
But this is ridiculous

JEROME: Don't you want it?

AYA: No
(Beat.)
Do I shock you?

JEROME: Of course not
Why would you?

AYA: You say these words easily because it is not your child

JEROME: I say these words easily because I know you
You

AYA: Look at me Jerome
My belly is soft already
Distended with life
Life is heavy on my shoulders

Burying me slowly

(Pause.)

This shouldn't have happened

(Almost to self.)

This should not have happened to me

JEROME: But it has Aya…

AYA: Jerome I can not be a mother

Not the type of mother I want to be

JEROME: But you can/

AYA: I can not be Leader and Mother

JEROME: I know

AYA: Outside of Shaktipur is genocide

A civil war – where the enemy lives within us

Girls cost too much, mean too little

Women's bodies open to receive, but are given nothing

And still the world (India) abides…

Mother used to say I had small hands and big eyes

Here – I could look as much as I wanted and take as much as I could carry:

In Shaktipur, I am not the legal or sexual property of any man

Here I have the chance to make a change

I ask for freedom; to value women not by their standards

But by our own…

It is not too much

Outside these foundations are so hard to build

When the land is filled with stones

Hard stones of subjugation

They slip and slide into everyone's shoes

But they do not feel them digging into their skin anymore!

And carry on walking; taking the pain with them

To Lead I must have an unyielding and single voice
More powerful than prejudice and what has come before
Tell me how, if I compromise myself to *this?*
To this child, to motherhood, to this other life?
My vision distracted, diluted, divided?
No, these stones must be unearthed and dug up
Smashed and churned into a soft sand
So the feet of women can run free

Lights down. End of Act One.

ACT TWO

SCENE 1: SACRIFICE

AYA holds a long knife in her hand. OMAR prepares flowers, a small container of water and kunku (red powder) with incense. Sense of anticipation, excitement.

AYA: The Goddess Kali has blessed us on this day

OMAR: I would like to speak Aya

AYA: If you wish, although it is not necessary

OMAR: You have said my time devoted to the gardens, bore fruit

And Sem he has produced this feast

He has tended the lamb

Let me do what is right

AYA: You might think that what I ask you to do is a measure of how I love you.

But think a little harder.

SEM: It's OK Aya…

I agree. This should be Omar's honour

AYA begins to sharpen the knife. She says a prayer. The men wait.

OMAR: But brother, if you wish it to be you…

SEM: No, no. Not me

Only if Aya wishes it

AYA: As you know, the honour of sacrificing the lamb is not to be taken lightly

It is said to be the task of the favourite husband in some families

In others, the task of the newest husbands

Sometimes, the task of the least squeamish

We must all find our own path

…

Truth is, you have both had a chance

Had a time…

So it is harder than usual

OMAR pushes forward a little, ready to take the knife.

AYA: This time we have been blessed with someone with a desire to learn more

OMAR: /I do Aya.

AYA: Be part of this community, despite his difficulties with understanding.

Sometimes we may feel compelled to misunderstand ignorance for lack of interest.

But ignorance simply asks for knowledge. It is an opportunity.

AYA hesitates. Looking at OMAR.

OMAR: I will do my best Aya.

AYA: This decision does not mean I care less for the other.

But I must do what is right. For everyone.

Jerome….

JEROME doesn't move. AYA lifts the knife and points it to him.

AYA: Take it

JEROME steps forward unwillingly.

OMAR: A stranger?!

AYA places the knife in his hands. He takes it slowly, feeling the power.

AYA: A stranger to take the burden from both of you

SEM: Aya please!

AYA: It is what I don't ask you to do, that is the true measure.

You forget that today is also the day for wives to honour and thank our husbands for what they give us

This is my gift to you…

SEM: Aya. Please! He doesn't know what to do…

OMAR: Aya… If you can not choose one of your husbands

What use are we?

How will he do this Aya?

He is not a man of the land

JEROME: Aya. I am flattered but/

AYA: You will do this Jerome

    As we discussed

OMAR: Aya look at him. He's afraid!

JEROME: Not afraid

OMAR: How will he kill the lamb?

JEROME: *(Unsure.)* I am not afraid

OMAR: Can you take a lamb; slice her throat?

    Tie her legs to the tree...Watch the blood run out onto the ground

    Then gaze into those eyes and wonder, what would she have been?

    Beat. Both men see the dead lamb.

JEROME: *(Shaken.)* Aya, its true I've never killed before

    Please/

OMAR: *(Composed.)* I can tell.

AYA: He can do it

    Jerome, I am asking you to do this

JEROME: Of course, but/

AYA: You wanted to know about this life

    About my house

JEROME: Surely someone should watch?

AYA: It must be done *alone*

    It is the job of a man to commune

    As nature and survival conspire to be one

SEM: Let me help him...

    SEM brings over the tray.

OMAR: So you just let him? As if he is one of us?

AYA: Jerome will do this.

OMAR: How can a stranger walk in and take our place

    So easily?

SEM: Aya – The lamb hasn't been blessed/

OMAR: Will you give him

Everything he wants?

AYA: It doesn't matter!

SEM: The Goddess will be angry.

AYA: Sem! A sacrifice is a sacrifice.

In the end, the animal will be dead.

Shock at AYA's callousness. SEM distraught, leaves. AYA presses the knife into his hands.

AYA: Go Jerome! Now!

JEROME exits. SEM takes the tray with him.

AYA and OMAR watch JEROME walk out into the fields. AYA tries to embrace OMAR.

AYA: So the killing of a life means so much to you?

OMAR: You disrespect me like that in front of a ferenghi?

AYA: I want to teach him

OMAR: What? How to be your husband?

AYA: He wants to know so much about this life

He thinks he knows it

Understands it

Now let him feel it

OMAR: You should have sent him away

AYA: You know we can't turn out people today

OMAR: So this?

Sending an unclean to do the sacrifice?

Breaking Sem's heart

Aya, what are you thinking?!

AYA: *(Angry.)* What do you think?

(Beat.)

My love, I'm thinking of both of you

OMAR: No Aya

AYA: Let him see what this is like

Then he will leave on his own accord

OMAR: I don't trust him

AYA: If we turn him out

He will only come back

I know his kind

OMAR: If you'd let me/

AYA: It would make it worse

Let me do it my way

OMAR: Your way Aya?

Haven't we had enough of your way?

SEM enters in a hurry. He searches desperately for anther knife.

AYA: What happened?

JEROME enters, running also, carrying the knife. His hands and clothes are covered in blood. OMAR goes to JEROME.

OMAR: What happened…?

JEROME: *(Panting.)* I tried to do it.

But she's still moving.

Breathing. Writhing.

I don't know if it's still alive…

OMAR: Where is she?!

JEROME: She's in pain.

The sound of it, it's horrible

OMAR: Where is she?!

JEROME: In the pasture…

OMAR: You just left her…?!

OMAR takes the knife. JEROME is in shock. SEM stands up, alert.

OMAR: *(Pulling JEROME away.)* Show me….

OMAR and JEROME exit. AYA and SEM wait. Sound of the lamb being killed.

SEM: I blessed the lamb

AYA: What?

SEM: I got everything…

The flowers, the water, the kunku.

All for the blessing you didn't want…

I found her sleeping in the corner

Her eyes afraid…

AYA: *(Cold.)* I told you not/…

SEM: I did what was right

>   For all of us

>   *OMAR returns, JEROME on his heels.*

OMAR: *(To JEROME.)* He's ruined it!!

AYA: Leave it

>   It's done

OMAR: The body was mauled by the inexperienced hand you sent

>   The slow death you gave her so you could set your example

>   We didn't even bless her

AYA: She was blessed. Sem blessed the lamb

OMAR: It was cruelty at best

>   *SEM gets some rope for the lamb.*

SEM: *(Distraught.)* Brother, let us finish the task

>   *OMAR helps SEM. The men look at AYA accusingly.*

OMAR: *(Shaking head.)* He has ruined everything

>   And you do not even realise

>   *OMAR and SEM exit to get the lamb.*

JEROME: *(Shaken.)* I tried my best

AYA: I know you did

>   *Finally JEROME runs out to join the men.*

SCENE 2: BREAKING THE FAST

Late afternoon, kitchen. Lamb's head on the table. Blood on the floor. OMAR and SEM are cutting up the rest of the meat slowly and methodically. OMAR is very skilled. The heat rises through this scene to unbearable levels as the midday sun reaches its peak. On the stove onions are ready for the lamb.

OMAR: We did well with the lamb…

>   *Picking up a piece.*

SEM: Salt

OMAR passes the salt. SEM mixes it vigorously.

OMAR: Gentle brother

SEM: Where's the masala?

OMAR passes the masala to SEM, who tips it in rather carelessly.

OMAR: The blood cleared easily

JEROME enters – changing his shirt.

JEROME: It was almost blue on the ground

OMAR: Blood changes colour in death
but your hands trembled all the way

JEROME: I didn't expect/

OMAR: No

JEROME: You did it so fast. Cutting the lamb and even - oh the *head*
What will you do with it?

SEM: Have you come to help?

JEROME: Yes.
Yes, I have

SEM: If you want to help – start with the head

JEROME: Just tell me what you want me to do
I want to help

OMAR: Why – so eager?
Do not make yourself so at home Professor

JEROME: Your hostility is/

SEM: Take the head and remove the brains. *Here*
JEROME hesitates.

OMAR: Or perhaps you would like to teach Sem how to do it?

JEROME: I wouldn't conceive of/

OMAR: Why not? You already feel like one of us don't you?

SEM: You can not undo what you did to the lamb

JEROME: It wasn't my fault
I did my best

OMAR: If the task was too big

You should have admitted it

JEROME: Like you?

SEM: Why not?

JEROME: The two of you with this quasi-brotherhood

Cosy, little family who can not admit the truth

Even to yourselves?

OMAR: Which is?

JEROME: If you want to know/

OMAR: What would we not understand *Sahib*?

JEROME: Forget it

(He fans himself.)

The deed is done

Let us move on from it

OMAR: You speak as if you know the significance of what has happened

SEM: We can not 'move on' when something has been undone

JEROME: Perhaps you are being a little dramatic

OMAR: I know what you think so

That is why you can not be part of this life

JEROME: You think you know me

But you don't see anything

SEM: What does that mean?

JEROME: You don't see your wife, not really/

OMAR: Whatever you believe about what Aya wants of you

You will never be part of this

AYA enters, jubilant. Smiling, she sings, carrying some spices to add to the masala.

AYA: Some saffron, to give the scent of flowers

She dips her finger into the masala and tastes it, then pulls out some cinnamon and cloves.

AYA: Plenty of cloves and cinnamon to make it warm and fragrant.

Pleased, she mixes the masala once more and tastes. She puts the lamb into the pot.

AYA: Sometimes it needs a little more

AYA spies JEROME.

AYA: You did well…

He smiles weakly

AYA: It was too much. I'm sorry.

JEROME: No, no Aya. If I disappointed you…

AYA: *(Shakes head.)* No you did not

Now your work is done

OMAR: Aya, I pray you will send him to wait at the temple

SEM: Yes Aya. He can not stay.

AYA: It's done now

Let us focus on the food for the festival

OMAR: Send him away now…

Now Aya

AYA: We will see

JEROME: *(Distraught.)* You will see?

(Beat.)

AYA: Yes.

Let us talk about it

JEROME: Are you sending me away?

AYA: I didn't say that

SEM: Surely he can not stay?!

AYA: Let me see

JEROME: So you leave me?

Use me and then send me out?

OMAR: She didn't use you old man!

You used her, pretending to come here/ (for the wedding.)

We all know what you want!

AYA: Leave him/

OMAR: Leave him?

Aya – what is this?

AYA: Maybe it wasn't quite right, but/

OMAR: *(Soft.)* What does he have that you want Aya?

AYA: *Nothing*

He has nothing that I want

Nothing

JEROME stares at AYA in disbelief.

SEM: It's better if he goes

SEM goes to get JEROME's bag

JEROME: Wait

JEROME goes to the lamb's head. He bends down. AYA doesn't dare to breathe.

JEROME: So you didn't see it Sem?

AYA looks at JEROME, afraid.

SEM: See?

JEROME: You saw the lamb was unwell.

Didn't you see the cut on the side of her neck?

SEM: I thought a dog maybe…

(Beat.)

JEROME: A cut so fine?

SEM looks at the lamb again.

JEROME: Your beautiful Aya

She did that

SEM: Why?

JEROME: Ask her

AYA: Stop it Jerome

SEM inspects the lamb's head, AYA tries to stop him. He sees the cut. Gasps.

JEROME: A cut so fine

No one would see…

SEM: You did

(Beat.)

Did, *that* to her Aya… ?

JEROME: Yes

Aya took her

And cut her gently behind the ear

AYA: She was in the barn

Soft and full of sleep

JEROME: She took the blood, to fill her sacred bottle

AYA: It was only a little. Just enough to…

SEM: Smear it on our necks!

(Beat.)

Lie to us!

You smeared the blood of an animal on us!

Of my lamb*?*

AYA: *(Defiant but quiet.)* Yes

Pause. SEM looks AYA in the eye. Very still.

JEROME: *(Quiet.)* Aya is pregnant

OMAR: Aya?

SEM: Aya you have a baby in your belly

AYA nods.

OMAR dances, praises the Gods. Kisses the ground, then AYA, touches her feet. SEM follows suit.

OMAR: Our baby

Our child

New life!

AYA: Wait, wait!

OMAR and SEM sing louder and louder – elated. JEROME watches in horror. The men pick AYA up and dance. AYA tries to smile but she is terrified.

Eventually they set her down. OMAR hurriedly washes his hands and sets some fruit and presents it to AYA.

OMAR: Eat my love, eat!

AYA: I'm not hungry

OMAR: How can that be?

The baby needs food

Nourishment straight from the mother

To her heart

OMAR sings enthusiastically, beckoning SEM to join in. He finds some lime juice and mixes in the sugar syrup and makes one for each of them. Calling SEM to sit and making the three of them clink glasses.

OMAR: Brother, at the festival tonight we give thanks

For both for our wife, and child!

But also the annulled marriage

And our home intact

AYA ignores the food and looks to SEM. SEM takes a banana from AYA's plate. He meets AYA's gaze, but does not move. He picks up the banana and peels it. SEM slowly puts it in his mouth, blatantly breaking his fast. Tears roll down his face.

OMAR: Brother!

SEM: I have nothing to fast for

Not anymore

OMAR tries to stop SEM.

AYA: Leave it

They watch as SEM finishes the banana.

AYA: Do you think she suffered?

(Beat.)

The lamb. She trusted me…

SEM: We need to cancel the wedding

OMAR: How pleased Mother will be!

AYA: *(To SEM.)* Remember when she was little we used to bring her into the house?

The others got so angry, but we used to sneak her in anyway?

Omar, would chase her out

She was so sweet and trusting…

OMAR: We must go to the coast

Visit my father with the good news

AYA: *(Dull.)* Yes

OMAR: /What do you say brother?

SEM: We will prepare the house for a blessing
    Start to/

OMAR: Oh brother! All that is to come
    Now we celebrate
    Give thanks!

JEROME: Perhaps Aya might want to/

OMAR: Sit down?
    Sleep?
    My love, ask me and it is yours
    Does your tongue desire something sweet?
    Salty? Spicy?
    Tell me, and let me serve you/

AYA: /I'm fine, Just
    Leave me be!

    OMAR is hurt but he says nothing.

SEM: You did hurt her Aya

AYA: Who?

SEM: The lamb. She trusted you
    Loved you even...
    But you betrayed her

    AYA is strung. OMAR watches – realization finally dawning.

OMAR: A baby that a stranger knew of before your Husbands?

SEM: You didn't want us to know
    You were going to betray us too

AYA: Wait, I/

JEROME: I think Aya was trying to figure this out
    Right Aya?

OMAR: What do you know?!

JEROME: Nothing of course
    Nothing at all, except Aya told me/

SEM: Shaktipur has been waiting for this moment

OMAR: *We* have waited for this moment

SEM: We need to tell Mother

AYA: *(Sarcastic.)* Yes, why not?

Where there's a plan for a prison

She'll put the bars in herself

OMAR: *(Shocked.)* Is that how you see it?

AYA: You know, I always said I wouldn't be like her… Mother.

Trapped in a series of loveless marriages

Keeping her status in a town where people think only of
having as many children as they can/

OMAR: What are you saying?

SEM: You said you wanted Shakitpur to succeed!/

Roll of thunder in the distance.

OMAR: /To have a family

Our family

AYA: *Your* dreams

A fiction of my husbands'

Desire

OMAR: So this is a lie?

SEM: There is a *new life* in your belly

AYA: Oh Sem…

A new life?

Don't you see…

This new life

It will be your new life

(Pause… then very quiet.)

And the very end of mine…

(Long silence.)

SEM: The end?

AYA: Of everything I believe in

Everything I have worked for

(To OMAR.) Please, try to understand

This child doesn't belong here

JEROME: Aya… They can not force you.

You do not have to have it

AYA: *(Ignoring him and touching her stomach.)*

I can feel it

A tiny life flickering inside

Like a candle

Alight in the monsoon night

She's growing already…

Taking parts of me

Piecing it all together…

By herself

In the morning

She stirs up my insides

Bringing to the lips

The acid regurgitation

Of *my* dreams

Already she tells me…

Mother, you belong to me

SEM: *(Touching her stomach with tenderness.)* She is growing…

Trying to live

AYA: One month and already this?

SEM: *(Louder.)* Please stop Aya…

AYA: Sem, don't you see?

She is pulling me

Taking me somewhere I do not want to go

By the hand into the darkness

Calling me…

But…

(Beat.)

I don't want to be called…

Mother

She says

I'm coming…

SEM tries to loosen his hand from AYA, but she holds him firm. He starts to wince.

Sound of the procession outside in the distance getting closer throughout this next section.

SEM: The trousseau is on its way

JEROME: Just wait Omar

Give the lady a moment to gather herself

SEM: *(Worried.)* Aya?

OMAR: She is our Leader.

She does not 'gather' herself

AYA turns away. Roll of thunder closer.

AYA: I disappoint you

I disappoint myself

OMAR: What is it?

You don't want to nurse?

We will bring someone

Many women do not nurse

AYA: And watch another woman feed my child?

OMAR: Then feed her yourself!

AYA: I do not want to!

OMAR: Then what?

AYA: I do not want a child and then have to make allowances for it

Or not make allowances and let the guilt swallow me whole

Can't you see it will tear us apart?

OMAR: Then let me. I will bear all of it

(He bends down to AYA's feet.)

I will take care of her every need

I will feed, nurture and care for her

Aya, all I ask is let her come!

AYA: *(Shaking her head.)* For you I would do anything.

But this…

Once it's here I won't be able to turn away from it.

Can't you see that?

OMAR: *(Pause.)* You're ready for this.

Look at your body.

Your breasts, hips: Power and fragility.

All in one breath

(He bows his head.)

You're ready…

AYA: I love you Omar, but it doesn't mean I want to be a mother to your child.

(Beat.)

OMAR: *(Looking away.)* It is a waste!

AYA: *(Wounded.)* A waste! Waste?

Am I not enough?

You talk of loving me – but now all you want is this!

OMAR: Why do you say it like that Aya?

AYA: Because that is how I feel.

Because you and I have always told each other how we feel

OMAR: So why did you hide this?

(Beat.)

AYA: Because I didn't want to hurt you

OMAR: Because you were so sure?

So sure you wanted to murder our child?

AYA: *No!*

OMAR: *(Disgust.)* You are no different from the others outside

AYA: How can you say that?

(Beat.)

OMAR: You sang me a song to bring me here

Poems of forgotten girls, of betrayed women.

Serenaded me tales of lost girls and dreams

Made me live like this!!

AYA: A woman does not equal mother!

JEROME: *(Quiet.)* I see that Aya

OMAR: *(Gentle.)* Inside there is the blood of you and me.

The flesh of ours

Do you want to pull it out and tear it apart?

Like a piece of fish skin for the cat?

AYA: Stop it

SEM: We'd all be guilty

JEROME: Of what? Considering her right?

It is she that will carry the baby.

Deliver and nurse it

OMAR: *(Cold, hurt.)* You are not the first

Nor the last woman to bring a child into this world Aya

AYA: What do you mean?

OMAR: You can speak

You can speak poetry

You can speak poetically and lament

You can do all of this

(Beat.)

But the deed is done Aya

Nature, has had her way with you

Rain on the roof.

Procession outside, sound of bell/ ankle bells announcing the trousseau has arrived.

SEM: The trousseau is here

(Beat.)

OMAR: Send them back

AYA: No

SEM: They are already unloading the boxes

OMAR: Send them away

AYA: Please my love

Just wait

OMAR: What for?

So you can carry on your lie?

SEM: What shall I tell them?

OMAR: The boxes will be of no use to you Aya

They will not take you to Mumbai

AYA exits. The men stare at each other.

AYA finally comes in struggling with a large box/suitcase.

OMAR: You shouldn't

He stops AYA and brings the box/suitcase himself. AYA and OMAR stare at each other.

AYA: *(To OMAR.)* You are right – these boxes won't take Shaktipur to Mumbai

Won't help us to continue our good work

But the marriage will…

AYA turns to carry more boxes. SEM helps.

SEM: The rain will destroy the boxes

We need to bring them in

OMAR: Leave them

SEM: People will talk brother

AYA: I can do it myself.

OMAR relents. Throughout this next section – OMAR and SEM are busy with the boxes and do not always hear what JEROME says to AYA.

JEROME: You can not use your body as a commodity Aya

AYA: The path may be wrong

But the destination is right

I am willing to walk it

SEM returns with a box.

JEROME: I think your husbands are unwilling to see your side

But whatever happens today, will be something new in this house…

Isn't that so Sem? You're very quiet

Perhaps you do not agree with your brother

Rain comes on stronger. OMAR enters with another box.

SEM: Aya must do what is right

Change must begin with you

AYA: But Sem can't you see?

Only a woman who does not desire her 'self'

Who can truly give herself to a child

Can be a real mother

The rest, they are imitating

(Beat.)

I can not give myself in that way to a man or a child

I belong, to myself

JEROME: To yourself or your community?

They are not the same thing

OMAR: Shut up

You think that you can step between us?

Sem is beyond a brother

We decide together

JEROME: You are not brothers

Not by blood

OMAR: Aya is the blood the binds us

Do you understand?!

JEROME: Aya, your husbands are no different from the others outside

AYA: On the veranda

Please leave the boxes on the veranda!

Thunder.

OMAR: She doesn't need you

She will never need you

SEM and OMAR exit.

JEROME: Come…

Come away with me

No more bickering husbands

No more restriction

We will go back to London/

 You will be free

AYA: London?

JEROME: I won't ask you for any children

You will be free to

Do whatever you want

AYA: And my wedding?

The plans for Shakitpur?

JEROME: There will be no suitor

You want your freedom, Aya darling

Then you have it

AYA turns away.

JEROME: It's simple Aya

You have a right to have a child

Or not

The right to marry

Or not

But not both

AYA: *(Bitter.)* You leave me with poor choices

JEROME: *(Wry, smiling.)* No poorer than mine

No doubt if you go to Mumbai for a termination

Your beloved Husbands will tell the village

So you must leave, as I must

AYA: So you'll trap me the same

Give me a gift of freedom in hand for a cage of another

JEROME: You will have a freedom of your body

AYA: I've seen this freedom of yours

Women working, rearing and managing

In your world, a woman must be all things

Despite her biology

(Beat.)

What you haven't realized is that a woman is bound to her child,

Whatever, wherever she is.

That no amount of 'emancipation' will 'free' her of that.

JEROME: So it's not good enough for you?

JEROME tries to touch AYA. She pushes him away.

JEROME: What is this place?

> With its rules?
>
> Treating women like Goddesses
>
> Chaining them to it the same?

AYA: And you?

> Treating women like 'equals'
>
> But punishing them for it?

JEROME: You don't know that

> Come Aya, calm down
>
> Think carefully

AYA: But I have thought.

> Of all of this, before

JEROME: You must see then; this isn't normal

AYA: *Normal?*

JEROME: This way of life

> Treating you like a piece of meat to breed
>
> A false freedom with a harem of men
>
> A life where a man and woman can not even promise themselves to each other
>
> Is that anyway to raise children?

AYA: *(Sarcastic.)* So I see you understand

> How this all works

JEROME: It isn't *working* Aya

> When even you
>
> Can't do what is expected of her
>
> *Rain comes on strong. Comes through the open windows.*

JEROME: This false sense of emancipation

> Will destroy you my love

AYA: No! What will destroy me is you

> Clothed in humility of understanding
>
> But the pulsing blood of superiority through your veins!
>
> *OMAR and SEM enter.*

JEROME: You will never change centuries of subjugation…

AYA: I will make it work

JEROME: *(Laughs.)* You will make it work?

> You, the Leader of this grand, great community:
>
> The Mother who does not want to Mother!
>
> *AYA slaps JEROME.*

AYA: Get out!

JEROME: You will fail Aya

> *OMAR pushes JEROME towards his bag. JEROME picks it up.*

JEROME: I did this all for you

> It was the only way you would see
>
> Face the truth
>
> *(Beat.)*
>
> I'm sorry Aya/

AYA: I believe you are

> But I see what you have done Jerome
>
> And you have done this all for yourself
>
> *Rain streams down. JEROME exits. He knocks over the food and festival arrangements, ruining everything.*
>
> *AYA exits. SEM and OMAR stare at each other in disbelief.*

SCENE 3: THE FINAL BARGAIN

Storm in full force. SEM and OMAR clear the mess that JEROME has left.

SEM: The women will be here soon.

> To take Aya for the ceremony
>
> *(Beat.)*
>
> Will you tell them?

OMAR: Yes

SEM: Aya is suffering

OMAR: Brother, do you remember the story of the woman who found the injured snake?

> She took it home and nursed it.
>
> She spent many nights, checking the bandages, feeding it with her own hands, bringing back its strength…

SEM: She is our wife

OMAR: And when it was well…

It bit her.

SEM: The woman was virtuous.

OMAR: And she said why, why did you do that?

And the snake said, I'm a snake!

and slithered off into the forest.

SEM: It's not so simple…

OMAR: Brother, love the snake for her smooth skin, her power

But know what it is you love

SEM: My love isn't ordinary.

It doesn't begin

And finish like a drink of water

OMAR: She has to do what is right

SEM: What of Shaktipur?

OMAR: You think of the village?

Instead of our home, our family?

SEM: She suffers

OMAR: Let her!

SEM: If she is not of good mind

Shaktipur will suffer

OMAR: And us? Brother, think of us!

Have we not wanted a child for so long?

SEM nods.

OMAR: This is the Goddess's doing

Besides are these not the rules

That Aya leads with?

AYA enters.

SEM: The food is destroyed Aya

We can not do anymore

AYA: So what?

Is there nothing more to be made?

Nothing to be done?

They ignore her.

AYA: Sem!

SEM: Aya, I'm sorry there is nothing more we can do

OMAR: There is nothing more to do

Except for us to prepare for us finally becoming fathers

Both of us becoming men at last!

AYA pours a drink for each of them.

AYA: Well let us celebrate

SEM: You shouldn't

AYA: Come now

Nature is stronger than a drop of alcohol

She takes a sip and then allows OMAR to take the glass away.

OMAR: It is nature

The force of the physical world.

You are at the centre of it

AYA: So I relent. So I give in to this.

This process that I can not see, or understand

To the principles that I believe in, but am too weak to fulfill

OMAR: Finally!

AYA: You are right

The child is yours and your right is to this child, anchored safe inside me. You are the wind that directs us, but I am the sea carrying and protecting it

We, the wind and sea, must make this journey together

OMAR: Finally you speak the truth

AYA: The truth – yes.

Your truth and mine are not the same thing

But we have a shared truth now

We will have this child, Omar

We will

But we travel with our eyes open

OMAR: They are open

AYA: For now.

For this moment as I carry this promise for you…

And what when you unwrap it my love and find a beating heart that yearns for you?

How will you remember me then?

SEM: But Aya, there are two of us

AYA: Oh Sem. You are a father to this child as much as Omar

You will melt and delight in it

You will smile even when you are angry with me…

You will take its hand instead of mine

OMAR: What do you expect? We will be fathers as you will be a mother

SEM: You will do the same Aya.

You will fall in love again.

This time, truly deeply

With not a man, but a child

AYA: *This (Meaning them.)* place is not enough for me.

OMAR: What are you saying?

AYA: You have what you want.

A child, a family. Let me/

SEM: Marry tonight?

AYA: And why not?

It is no different than/

If you found out, after the wedding

SEM: So you wished to marry with a child in your belly?

AYA: If you knew tomorrow instead of today? What then?

SEM: No one will believe it

AYA: Of course they will. These things happen.

I will make it happen.

SEM: Nothing will change Aya

AYA: *(Calm.)* I will drown in milk of motherhood

Don't you see Sem?

Yes I am afraid

Afraid of what I will become

Not just you and me.
All of us
Everything
Do you want that?

OMAR: Every woman here must bear

AYA: Yes, these are the rules
The foundation of what we believe here
But what about me?
The woman you love?

OMAR: Fine! Is that what you want?
To sleep with another man?

AYA: Desire? Is that what you think this is for?
Desire is that rush of fluid in your mouth
Right before you take your first bite
This is survival I ask for
Not some fantasy
Listen to me Omar
I will have this child
If this is what you want
But give me something in return…

SEM: And another man? What does he do for you?

AYA: To him I am not a wife or a mother.
To him I am Aya
With him and the people
I will take Shaktipur to the city

OMAR: And us?

AYA: *(Tender.)* I am everything you need
Love, mother, wife.
All things will be tied to the domestic umbilicus.
The heart that feed this child,
will also swell and feed you all.

Pause, as they all consider.

OMAR: No

AYA: No? You would deny me this?

Us, all of us this?

Destroy me, as they destroy those outside?

OMAR: *(Wavering.)* It is not the same

AYA: Nobody else can do this my love

Nobody can take our teaching to the city

SEM: She is right

AYA: What will become of us here?

Secluded in the middle of nowhere

Our cause lost in the rice fields?

OMAR: I don't care about that! Not now.

AYA: This is not about the baby, this is about your possession

OMAR: What possession?

AYA: Me

OMAR: *(Laughing.)* This is not about the baby

This is about your ambition Aya

You put everything behind that

AYA: Yes. Even myself!

SEM: But Aya

AYA: This way of the world is not right

We can not create change if we keep conceding

SEM: A child is not a concession

AYA: You are not listening to me!

OMAR: Come on Sem

Beat. SEM does not move.

AYA: And now you want to run to Mother

Like small boys?

OMAR hesitates.

OMAR: *(Low, controlled.)* Fine.

Have what you want

When the baby is born

I'll take care of her

Aya, you can have a new husband,

Take your new life…

But not me…

Not anymore Aya.

AYA: *(Recoiling, falling.)* You will just discard me?

He touches her stomach.

OMAR: This is your choice Aya. Take it.

AYA: Not like this

OMAR: I can not be with a woman who rejects her child

A mother who rejects my child

You want to discard the gift that has been given to you

So I take back the only thing I have, my heart

(Beat.)

We will live together

A mother and father for this child

But I will never sleep in your bed again

(Beat.)

AYA: *(Sad.)* So you'll take your choice

As I've taken mine

Rain subsides. SEM and OMAR complete clearing up.

SCENE 4: DRESSING THE BRIDE

Dusk: Bedroom. OMAR and SEM have laid out the wedding sari, jewellery and flowers.

AYA enters. She is exhausted, but strong. She smiles at both of them despite the struggle. She is dressed in a petticoat and sari blouse. They bring in the new wedding sari in white, red and gold.

They wrap it around her, tucking in the pleats, and pulling it over her shoulder.

Next they adorn her with jewellery.

When they are finished they bow before her; she the beautiful bride. It is almost tender on SEM's part. Sad, deeply sad for OMAR.

SCENE 5: THE NEW LEADER

Lights up: Bedroom. There is the glow of a sunset. Sounds of the festival procession, as they get increasingly closer to the house.

AYA is dressed and waiting. Nervous. She clasps in her hand the SACRED BOTTLE with the lamb's blood.

SEM: The women are almost here

AYA: I am ready

SEM: Are you happy?

    With your decision?

AYA: *(Sighing.)* This is what is best

    He gives AYA the gold chain and nut.

SEM: *(Slowly and painfully.)*

    Aya you are not a mother

    You can not mother

AYA: Why do you say this now?

SEM: You will wither like a parched leaf

    AYA stares at him until he breaks her gaze.

AYA: I have to do this Sem

SEM: Yes, but you will only survive

    Not live

    When this baby arrives

    There will no joy in her mother's milk

AYA: /I will love it

    In my own way

SEM: Not concern that rocks it to sleep

    Nor loving eyes that watch her dream

AYA: /She will have her fathers

    Grandmothers, aunts and cousins/

SEM: It is not enough

AYA: What do you mean?

SEM: *(Trembling.)* Let us go to the city

    Find a doctor/

AYA: No Sem!

SEM: We can go tonight…

AYA: It is too late…

    I can not/

SEM: Why not?

AYA: Everything here is willing, able

    For me to have this child

    Even my body has disobeyed me

    So…

    SEM realization.

SEM: /So you do it *regardless?*

    (Beat.)

AYA: Yes. I do it because I must

SEM: *(Shaking head sadly.)* I do, because *I believe*

    You do, because you must believe

AYA: I follow the way

SEM: Whose way is *this Aya?!*

    AYA kisses SEM.

AYA: You think me cruel

    You think me less of a woman

    Yes?

    SEM says nothing.

AYA: It is not on your tongue, but in your heart

    In your eyes

    SEM tries to smile, but fails.

AYA: But this will make a difference

    I have to do this

    You have to believe me/

SEM: Everything I believed in…

    Everything *we* believed in*:*

    Shaktipur; the land, creating *something*

    …

    It means *nothing* if you don't really believe

AYA: How can you say that? Sem you know/

SEM: A leader with *no* faith, is worse than a leader with the *wrong* faith

You will lead this community into darkness

AYA: You don't know/

SEM: If you can lie to us. What will you do to them?

Those that believe you? Trust you?

AYA: This is the *only way*

OMAR enters carrying the two garlands. Watches.

SEM: I see you Aya

All of you

And I love it

But, this I can not do

AYA: Can not do what?

SEM: Watch you do this: to Omar, to me, to the community

I can not stay, in *my home,* anymore

AYA: What are you saying?

AYA begins to cry. SEM takes off his gold chain.

SEM: When it's morning,

Ask Omar to take the wedding sheets

(Beat.)

I won't be here

AYA begins to cry. SEM too. He begins to leave.

AYA: Wait!

AYA takes off the SACRED BOTTLE. Slowly, she pours the blood onto the floor and drops it to the ground. SEM tries to stop her.

SEM: What are you doing Aya?!

AYA: There will be no lie

If they want a Leader

Let me lead

SEM: They will refuse you/

AYA: I will not lie

I will not deceive my people

SEM: Aya, they won't let you

AYA: Our value will be more than just mother

    Breeder, producer of children

    (Beat.)

    This is where we went wrong in the first place

    We must be more than that

SEM: They will not understand/

AYA: And when we are mothers then let us understand, what
    that choice is

    With honesty

    SEM tries to speak

AYA: Shh. Let me.

    Let me speak my truth...

    AYA takes OMAR's hand.

AYA: Let the people decide …

    …What is right, right for this, for all of us

    SEM nods his head. AYA takes his hand.

AYA: Come. Let us go…

    Lights bright and strong. Sound of women singing rises.

    *Defiant, AYA leads the men out. She steps over the empty bottle on
    the floor. SEM close behind, OMAR following.*

    The End.